T0224244

Automatic Disambiguation of Author Names in Bibliographic Repositories

Synthesis Lectures on Information Concepts, Retrieval, and Services

Editor
Gary Marchionini, *University of North Carolina, Chapel Hill*

Synthesis Lectures on Information Concepts, Retrieval, and Services publishes short books on topics pertaining to information science and applications of technology to information discovery, production, distribution, and management. Potential topics include: data models, indexing theory and algorithms, classification, information architecture, information economics, privacy and identity, scholarly communication, bibliometrics and webometrics, personal information management, human information behavior, digital libraries, archives and preservation, cultural informatics, information retrieval evaluation, data fusion, relevance feedback, recommendation systems, question answering, natural language processing for retrieval, text summarization, multimedia retrieval, multilingual retrieval, and exploratory search.

Predicting Information Retrieval Performance
Robert M. Losee
2018

Framing Privacy in Digital Collections with Ethical Decision Making
Virginia Dressler
2018

Mobile Search Behaviors: An In-depth Analysis Based on Contexts, APPs, and Devices
Dan Wu and Shaobo Liang
2018

Images in Social Media: Categorization and Organization of Images and Their Collections
Susanne Ørnager and Haakon Lund
2018

Exploring Context in Information Behavior: Seeker, Situation, Surroundings, and Shared
Identities
Naresh Kumar Agarwal
2017

Researching Serendipity in Digital Information Environments
Lori McCay-Peet and Elaine G. Toms
2017

Social Monitoring for Public Health
Michael J. Paul and Mark Dredze
2017

Digital Libraries for Cultural Heritage: Development, Outcomes, and Challenges from
European Perspectives
Tatjana Aparac-Jelšić
2017

iRODS Primer 2: Integrated Rule-Oriented Data System
Hao Xu, Terrell Russell, Jason Coposky, Arcot Rajasekar, Reagan Moore, Antoine de Torcy,
Michael Wan, Wayne Shroeder, and Sheau-Yen Chen
2017

Information Architecture: The Design and Integration of Information Spaces, Second
Edition
Wei Ding, Xia Lin, and Michael Zarro
2017

Fuzzy Information Retrieval
Donald H. Kraft and Erin Colvin
2017

Information Architecture: The Design and Integration of Information Spaces
Wei Ding and Xia Lin
2009

Reading and Writing the Electronic Book
Catherine C. Marshall
2009

Hypermedia Genes: An Evolutionary Perspective on Concepts, Models, and Architectures
Nuno M. Guimarães and Luís M. Carrico
2009

Understanding User-Web Interactions via Web Analytics
Bernard J. (Jim) Jansen
2009

XML Retrieval
Mounia Lalmas
2009

Faceted Search
Daniel Tunkelang
2009

Introduction to Webometrics: Quantitative Web Research for the Social Sciences
Michael Thelwall
2009

Exploratory Search: Beyond the Query-Response Paradigm
Ryen W. White and Resa A. Roth
2009

New Concepts in Digital Reference
R. David Lankes
2009

Automated Metadata in Multimedia Information Systems: Creation, Refinement, Use in Surrogates, and Evaluation
Michael G. Christel
2009

© Springer Nature Switzerland AG 2022

Reprint of original edition © Morgan & Claypool 2020

All rights reserved. No part of this publication may be reproduced, stored in a retrieval system, or transmitted in any form or by any means—electronic, mechanical, photocopy, recording, or any other except for brief quotations in printed reviews, without the prior permission of the publisher.

Automatic Disambiguation of Author Names in Bibliographic Repositories

Anderson A. Ferreira, Marcos André Gonçalves, and Alberto H. F. Laender

ISBN: 978-3-031-01194-8   paperback
ISBN: 978-3-031-02322-4   ebook
ISBN: 978-3-031-00229-8   hardcover

DOI 10.1007/978-3-031-02322-4

A Publication in the Springer series
SYNTHESIS LECTURES ON INFORMATION CONCEPTS, RETRIEVAL, AND SERVICES

Lecture #70
Series Editor: Gary Marchionini, *University of North Carolina, Chapel Hill*
Series ISSN
Print 1947-945X   Electronic 1947-9468

Automatic Disambiguation of Author Names in Bibliographic Repositories

Anderson A. Ferreira
Universidade Federal de Ouro Preto, Brazil

Marcos André Gonçalves
Universidade Federal de Minas Gerais, Brazil

Alberto H. F. Laender
Universidade Federal de Minas Gerais, Brazil

SYNTHESIS LECTURES ON INFORMATION CONCEPTS, RETRIEVAL, AND SERVICES #70

ABSTRACT

This book deals with a hard problem that is inherent to human language: ambiguity. In particular, we focus on author name ambiguity, a type of ambiguity that exists in digital bibliographic repositories, which occurs when an author publishes works under distinct names or distinct authors publish works under similar names. This problem may be caused by a number of reasons, including the lack of standards and common practices, and the decentralized generation of bibliographic content. As a consequence, the quality of the main services of digital bibliographic repositories such as search, browsing, and recommendation may be severely affected by author name ambiguity. The focal point of the book is on automatic methods, since manual solutions do not scale to the size of the current repositories or the speed in which they are updated. Accordingly, we provide an ample view on the problem of automatic disambiguation of author names, summarizing the results of more than a decade of research on this topic conducted by our group, which were reported in more than a dozen publications that received over 900 citations so far, according to Google Scholar. We start by discussing its motivational issues (Chapter 1). Next, we formally define the author name disambiguation task (Chapter 2) and use this formalization to provide a brief, taxonomically organized, overview of the literature on the topic (Chapter 3). We then organize, summarize and integrate the efforts of our own group on developing solutions for the problem that have historically produced state-of-the-art (by the time of their proposals) results in terms of the quality of the disambiguation results. Thus, Chapter 4 covers HHC - Heuristic-based Clustering, an author name disambiguation method that is based on two specific real-world assumptions regarding scientific authorship. Then, Chapter 5 describes SAND - Self-training Author Name Disambiguator and Chapter 6 presents two incremental author name disambiguation methods, namely INDi - Incremental Unsupervised Name Disambiguation and INC- Incremental Nearest Cluster. Finally, Chapter 7 provides an overview of recent author name disambiguation methods that address new specific approaches such as graph-based representations, alternative predefined similarity functions, visualization facilities and approaches based on artificial neural networks. The chapters are followed by three appendices that cover, respectively: (i) a pattern matching function for comparing proper names and used by some of the methods addressed in this book; (ii) a tool for generating synthetic collections of citation records for distinct experimental tasks; and (iii) a number of datasets commonly used to evaluate author name disambiguation methods. In summary, the book organizes a large body of knowledge and work in the area of author name disambiguation in the last decade, hoping to consolidate a solid basis for future developments in the field.

KEYWORDS

heuristic-based clustering, self-training author name disambiguation, incremental unsubervised name disambiguation, incremental nearest cluster, automatic disambiguation

To our families,
with love.

Contents

Preface

Ambiguity is an inherent part of the human language and is expected that systems that process natural language will suffer with this problem, mainly regarding the quality of the services they provide. This is exactly the case of digital repositories of bibliographic information, which store for long periods of time data about the scientific and technical production (aka, as works) of (groups of) individuals and institutions in the form of *bibliographic citation records*.

One of the main, and most difficult to solve, types of ambiguity that exist in these digital bibliographic repositories is *author name ambiguity*, which occurs when an author publishes works under distinct names or distinct authors publish works under similar names. This problem may be caused by a number of reasons, including the lack of standards and common practices, and the decentralized generation of bibliographic content. As a consequence, the quality of the main services of digital bibliographic repositories such as search, browsing, and recommendation may be severely affected by author name ambiguity.

The challenges of dealing with the author name ambiguity have led to a myriad of disambiguation methods. Notice that here our focus is on automatic methods, since manual solutions do not scale to the size of the current repositories or the speed in which they are updated.

Accordingly, in this book we provide an ample view on the problem of *automatic disambiguation of author names*, summarizing the results of more than a decade of research on this topic conducted by our group, which were reported in more than a dozen publications that received over 900 citations so far, according to Google Scholar. We start by discussing its motivational issues (Chapter 1). Next, we formally define the *author name disambiguation task* (Chapter 2) and use this formalization to provide a brief, taxonomically organized, overview of the literature on the topic (Chapter 3).

We then organize, summarize, and integrate the efforts of our own group on developing solutions for the problem that have historically produced state-of-the-art (by the time of their proposals) results in terms of the quality of the disambiguation results as formally measured by several domain-specific evaluation metrics (see Section 2.3 for a discussion on these metrics). More specifically, Chapter 4 covers *HHC - Heuristic-based Clustering*, an author name disambiguation method that is based on two specific real-world assumptions regarding scientific authorship. Then, Chapter 5 describes *SAND - Self-training Author Name Disambiguator* and Chapter 6 presents two incremental author name disambiguation methods, namely *INDi - Incremental Unsupervised Name Disambiguation* and *INC - Incremental Nearest Cluster*. Each one of these methods is first introduced by means of an illustrative example, before their implementation details are properly described by specific algorithms.

Finally, Chapter 7 provides an overview of recent author name disambiguation methods that address new specific approaches such as graph-based representations, alternative predefined similarity functions, visualization facilities, and approaches based on artificial neural networks, a trend in the area.

This last chapter is followed by three appendices that cover, respectively: (a) the Fragment Comparison Function, a specific pattern matching function for comparing proper names and used by some of the methods addressed in this book; (b) SyGAR – Synthetic Generator of Authorship Records, a tool for generating synthetic collections of citation records for distinct experimental tasks; and (c) a number of datasets commonly used to evaluate author name disambiguation methods.

As far as we know, this is the largest and most comprehensive compilation of specific issues and solutions for the author name disambiguation problem, and we sincerely hope that this compilation will be useful for those working or intending to work on this challenging but very important problem. Finally, we would like to thank all our former students that directly and indirectly contributed to this book, here represented by Ricardo G. Cota, coauthor of Chapter 4, and Ana Paula de Carvalho and Alan Filipe Santana, coauthors of Chapter 6. We also thank the support provided by our institutions and the research grants received from CAPES, CNPq, and FAPEMIG.

Anderson A. Ferreira, Marcos André Gonçalves, and Alberto H. F. Laender
Belo Horizonte, April 2020

CHAPTER 1

Introduction

Several bibliographic repositories, such as DBLP,[1] CiteSeer,[2] PubMed,[3] and BDBComp,[4] provide features and services that facilitate literature research and discovery as well as other types of functionality. Such systems may list millions of bibliographic citation records (here understood as a set of bibliographic attributes such as author and coauthor names, work and publication venue titles of a particular publication) and have become an important source of information for academic communities since they allow the search and discovery of relevant publications in a centralized manner. Also, studies based on digital library content can lead to interesting results such as coverage of topics, research tendencies, quality and impact of publications of a specific sub-community or individuals, patterns of collaboration in social networks, etc. This kind of information, which is used, for instance, by funding agencies on decisions for grants and for individuals' promotions, presuppose *high quality content* [Laender et al., 2008, Lee et al., 2007].

According to Lee et al. [2007], the challenges to have high quality content comes from data-entry errors, citation formats, lack of (enforcement of) standards, imperfect citation-gathering software, ambiguous author names, abbreviations of publication venue titles, and large-scale citation data. Among these challenges, *ambiguous author names* have attracted a lot of attention from the digital library research community due to its inherent difficulty. Specifically, author name ambiguity occurs when a set of citation records contains author names that are ambiguous and cannot be properly identified, i.e., the same author may appear under distinct names (synonyms), or distinct authors may have similar names (homonyms). This problem may be caused by a number of reasons [McKay et al., 2010], including name changes due to personal circumstances [Gomide et al., 2017a], variation in transliteration of non-Roman names, typographical errors, lack of standards and common practices, and decentralized generation of content (i.e., by means of automatic harvesting [Lagoze and de Sompel, 2001]).

An interesting example that illustrates how author name ambiguity impacts the content of a bibliographic repository can be taken from a previous version of DBLP. In that version, if one searched for the author name "Mohammed Zaki," the result would include three name variations: "Mohammed Zaki," "Mohammed J. Zaki," and "Mohammed Javeed Zaki" (see Figure 1.1). Although all three names seemed to refer to the same person, they in fact illustrate a case that involved both synonyms and homonyms. While the first name referred to Mohammed

---

[1] https://dblp.org
[2] http://citeseerx.ist.psu.edu/index
[3] https://www.ncbi.nlm.nih.gov/pubmed
[4] http://www.lbd.dcc.ufmg.br/bdbcomp

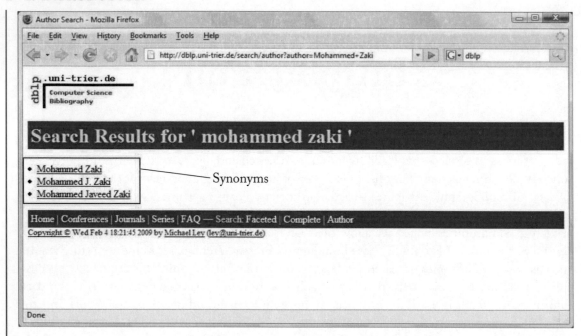

Figure 1.1: Synonyms: a unique author with several name variations.

Zaki from the Systems and Computer Engineering Department at the Al-Azhar University in Nasr City, Cairo, Egypt, the second and third names referred to Mohammed Zaki from the Department of Computer Science at the Rensselaer Polytechnic Institute in Troy, New York, USA, thus characterizing a synonym case.

However, by clicking on the "Mohammed Zaki" link the result page (see Figure 1.2) showed an example of a homonym, since the returned page actually refered to Mohammed Zaki from the Systems and Computer Engineering Department at the Al-Azhar University in Naar City, Egipt. Moreover, the second reference was actually coauthored by Mohammed Javeed Zaki from the Department of Computer Science at the Rensselaer Polytechnic Institute in the USA. Although in this case the problem was caused by different variations of an author's name, there are many other cases in which two different authors simply have exactly the same name, a common situation, for example, for authors with Asian names.

To show how the author name ambiguity problem requires a full time attention from digital library administrators, Figure 1.3 shows the results of a more recent search for the name "Mohammed Zaki" on DBLP. As one can see, this search returned six distinct results, revealing new variations of the name "Mohammed Zaki" in the DBLP repository, which shows the need for effective methods to address this problem.

Providing effective methods for author name disambiguation is not a trivial task. In recent years, a countless number of such methods have been proposed for addressing this prob-

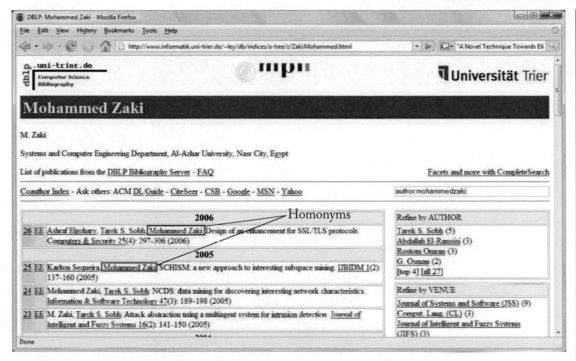

Figure 1.2: Homonyms: distinct authors with the same name variation.

lem [Ferreira et al., 2012b, Hussain and Asghar, 2017b, Smalheiser and Torvik, 2009], ranging from simple heuristic-based methods to more sophisticated ones based on machine learning and artificial intelligence techniques. Thus, before presenting some of them, we discuss motivational issues that have challenged the development of effective methods for automatic disambiguation of author names in bibliographic repositories.

1.1   MOTIVATIONAL ISSUES

There are several issues that need to be considered in order to produce reliable solutions to the author name disambiguation (AND) problem so that they can be employed in production mode in real bibliographic repositories [Ferreira, 2012, Ferreira et al., 2012b]. These issues may include: (i) intrinsic characteristics of the problem that can be considered invariants and any AND solution needs to consider; or (ii) open (research) problems for which there is still not a definite solution. For the sake of discussion in this book, we do not distinguish them, as we still consider all of them as motivation to continue working on the AND problem. Next, we briefly address several of them.

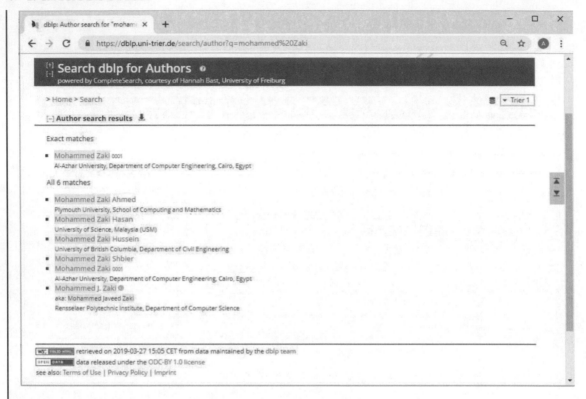

Figure 1.3: Recent search for Mohammed Zaki on DBLP.

Very Little Data in the Citations. In most cases we have only basic information about the citations available: author (coauthor) names, work and publication venue titles, and publication year. Furthermore, in some cases author names contain only the initial and the last surname, and the publication venue title is usually abbreviated. New strategies that try to derive implicit information (e.g., topics) or gather additional information from the Web are promising in this scenario.

Very Ambiguous Cases. Several methods exploit coauthor-based heuristics, by explicitly assuming the hypotheses that: (i) very rarely ambiguous references will have coauthors in common who have also ambiguous names; or (ii) it is rare that two authors with very similar names work in the same research area. These hypotheses work in most cases but, when they fail, the errors they generate are very hard to fix. For example, in the case of authors with Asian names, the first hypothesis fails much more frequently than for authors with English or Latin names.

Citations with Errors. Errors occur very often in citation data and are sometimes impossible to detect. Thus, disambiguation methods need to be tolerant to them.

Efficiency.   With the very large amount of works being published nowadays in different knowledge areas, current author name disambiguation methods need to deal with the problem efficiently. However, few of the proposed methods in the literature [de Carvalho et al., 2011, Liu et al., 2014, Santana et al., 2017] have this explicit concern.

Adaptability to Different Knowledge Areas.   As we shall see, most of the collections used to evaluate author name disambiguation methods are related to Computer Science. However, other knowledge areas, such as Humanities, Biology, and Medicine, may have different publication patterns (e.g., many publications with a sole author or with many coauthors), which may cause some additional difficulties for the current generation of methods, thus requiring adaptations.

Incremental Disambiguation.   Ideally, author name disambiguation should be performed incrementally as new citations are incorporated into a bibliographic repository, since it is not reasonable to assume that its entire repository should be disambiguated at each new load. However, the vast majority of the current disambiguation methods ignore this fact. Promising solutions to this specific issue have been proposed by de Carvalho et al. [2011] and Santana et al. [2017], and are addressed in Chapter 6. Despite that, current solutions still have some limitations and do not offer the flexibility required by most bibliographic services. Thus, there are still room for new methods to explore in this regard, before new and more effective solutions should be provided. For this reason, new methods should explore this approach more effectively to avoid the need of regularly processing high expensive disambiguation procedures in order to keep a bibliographic repository free of ambiguous citation records.

Author Profile Changes.   It is common that the research interests of an author change over time. This can happen for many reasons, for example, new collaborations, changes in a research group or institution, natural evolution of a research field, among others. These changes cause modifications in the model representing the authors' profile, thus causing difficulties for the author name disambiguation methods. A possible solution may involve retraining, but determining when to retrain a method is a challenge by itself. However, this issue has been largely ignored by existing author name disambiguation methods, opening plenty of opportunities for exploration by new methods.

New Ambiguous Authors.   Author name disambiguation methods should be capable of identifying references to new ambiguous authors who do not have citations in the digital library yet. However, very few reported methods [Santana et al., 2017, Veloso et al., 2012, Wang et al., 2020] have explicitly addressed this issue, which is known in other areas as the Open Set Recognition Problem [Scheirer et al., 2013], but has not been yet adequately addressed in the AND scenario.

Effectiveness.   Methods for disambiguating author names must be effective, i.e., they must correctly disambiguate the author names in bibliographic citations without affecting performance. Although many methods have been recently reported in the literature (see Chapter 3), there is still a lot of room for improvements with respect to effectiveness, as evidenced in comprehensive comparative studies [Santana et al., 2015, 2017].

Practicality and Cost.   Most of the best current methods for tackling the author name disambiguation problem are supervised, i.e., they require large amounts of manually labeled data explicitly indicating whether two ambiguous names correspond to the same author or not, or indicating the correct authors for the references. These labeled data serve as training for some machine learning procedure [Culotta et al., 2007, Han et al., 2015, 2004, Huang et al., 2006, Kim et al., 2019a, Torvik and Smalheiser, 2009, Treeratpituk and Lee Giles, 2009, Veloso et al., 2012]. However, creating such training data is very costly and laborious.[5] This also may hurt the practical application of these methods, particularly because bibliographic repositories evolve and more training is required to learn new patterns. In this regard, developing new solutions based on advanced machine learning techniques opens a new research scenario for more effective author name disambiguation methods [Ferreira et al., 2014, Kooli et al., 2018, Müller, 2017, Tran et al., 2014, Zhang et al., 2018].

Distinct Publication Patterns.   As we have already mentioned, most of the collections used to evaluate author name disambiguation methods are related to Computer Science. However, other knowledge areas (e.g., Humanities, Medicine, Geology and others) may have different publication patterns (e.g., publications with a sole author or with several coauthors) causing additional difficulties for the current generation of methods.

Evaluation.   Most methods for disambiguating author names in bibliographic citations have been evaluated in static scenarios without considering a time evolving repository, in which dynamic patterns such as the emergence of new authors and the change of researchers' interests/expertises over time impose a number of constraints [Ferreira et al., 2012a].

All these issues, by themselves, are hard to solve when considered in isolation. However, a practical AND method to be used in current bibliographic repositories need to deal with most of them at the same time. This demonstrates how difficult the AND problem is from both, the practical and scientific points of view.

Finally, it should be pointed out that author name disambiguation is not a problem only restricted to bibliographic repositories, but also affects other scenarios such as the case of patent corpuses [Kim et al., 2016, Li et al., 2014]. However, in this book we restrict our attention only to the former case, although some of the discussed solutions can be easily adapted to other contexts.

---

[5]It is fact that nowadays there is some amount of "semi-supervised training data" that could be considered at least as a "silver standard," such as ORCID data or records that have a match on email addresses. Although such data can help, they still do not solve the problem as their coverage is not complete, i.e., not all authors have an ORCID or can be unambiguously associated with something that resembles a unique ID, such as email addresses.

1.2   BOOK ORGANIZATION

The reminder of this book is organized as follows. Chapter 2 (*The Author Name Disambiguation Task – Foundations*) characterizes this important task by first presenting the definition of basic related concepts and then describing its main steps. It also describes some specific metrics usually adopted to assess the performance of existing author name disambiguation methods and discusses how these metrics are applied in practice. Then, Chapter 3 (*Taxonomy*) presents a taxonomy that we have proposed to classify existing author name disambiguation methods according to the type of approach they adopt and the evidence they explore in the disambiguation task. Next, Chapter 4 (*Heuristic-based Hierarchical Clustering Disambiguation*), Chapter 5 (*SAND: Self-training Author Name Disambiguator*), and Chapter 6 (*Incremental Author Name Disambiguation*) describe two author name disambiguation methods we have proposed and that explore distinct approaches according to our taxonomy. Finally, Chapter 7 (*Additional Methods for Author Name Disambiguation*) provides an overview of recent approaches to addressing the author name disambiguation problem, thus complementing the methods described in the previous chapters.

In addition, three appendices complement the material presented in this book. Appendix A describes the Fragment Comparison Function, a pattern matching function specially designed for comparing proper names that is used in some of the author name disambiguation methods described here. Then, Appendix B presents SyGAR, a tool for synthetic generation of authorship records that is very useful for the creation of synthetic collections of authorship records. As a final contribution, Appendix C describes a number of datasets that have been extensively used for evaluating several author name disambiguation methods proposed in the literature, some of which are presented in this book.

CHAPTER 2

The Author Name Disambiguation Task – Foundations

In this chapter, we characterize the author name disambiguation task. We start by presenting some basic definitions, followed by a brief description of the main steps involved in this task. Then, we present some of the evaluation metrics most used in the literature and briefly describe how they are applied to assess the performance of existing author name disambiguation methods.

2.1 BASIC DEFINITIONS

We start with some basic definitions aiming at providing a framework in order to characterize the author name disambiguation task. While presenting such definitions, we will refer to the bibliographic reference in Figure 2.1 as our running example.

Definition 2.1 (Citation Record). A citation record c is a list of bibliographic attributes, such as *authornames*, *worktitle*, *venuetitle*, *publicationyear*, etc., that describes a particular bibliographic reference (e.g., a conference paper or a journal article). Moreover, each citation record c includes at least the attributes *authornames* and *worktitle*. A specific value is associated with each attribute in a citation record, which may be composed of several elements. In case of the attribute *authornames*, each element corresponds to a specific part (e.g., first name or last surname) of the name of a single unique author. In the case of other attributes, an element corresponds to a word or term.

Table 2.1 shows the citation record derived from the bibliographic reference in Figure 2.1. Notice that, for providing an identification scheme, a *citation-id* attribute is added to each citation record.

Definition 2.2 (Authorship Record). An authorship record represents the participation of an author in a citation record c. Thus, if a citation record c has n authors, it generates n authorship records, one for each author. Each author name instance in a citation record refers to a specific author. Thus, we associate a list of attributes, such as *r.author*, *r.coauthors*, *r.worktitle*, *r.venuetitle*, and *r.publicationyear*, to each authorship record r. Thus, given a bibliographic citation with such attributes, they correspond, respectively, to the name of a specific author, the

> S. Godbole, I. Bhattacharya, A. Gupta, and A. Verma. (2010).
> Building re-usable dictionary repositories for real-world text
> mining. In *Proceedings of the 19th ACM international Con-
> ference on Information and Knowledge Management, CIKM
> 2010.* pages 1189–1198, Toronto, ON, Canada.

Figure 2.1: Example of a bibliographic reference.

Table 2.1: Example of a citation record

Attribute Name	Value
Citation-id	1
Authornames	S. Godbole, I. Bhattacharya, A. Gupta, A. Verma
Worktitle	Building re-usable dictionary repositories for real-world text mining
venuetitle	Proceedings of the 19th ACM International Conference on Information and Knowledge Management, CIKM 2010
Publicationyear	2010
Address	Toronto, ON, Canada
Pages	1189–1198

names of her coauthors, the title of the cited work and the respective publication year. Other relevant attributes such as *r.affiliation* and *r.e-mail* can be added to an authorship record to help the author name disambiguation task. However, here, we will refer only to the above attributes, since they are those usually found in the bibliographic citations.

Table 2.2 shows the authorship records r_1, r_2, r_3, and r_4 derived from the citation record shown in Table 2.1. For instance, looking at Table 2.2, we can see that the authorship record r_3 has the following attribute values: $r_3.author$="A. Gupta," $r_3.coauthors$={"S. Godbole," "I. Bhattacharya," "A. Verma"}, $r_3.worktitle$= "Building re-usable dictionary repositories for real-world text mining," $r_3.venuetitle$= "Proceedings of the 19th ACM International Conference on Information and Knowledge Management, CIKM 2010" and $r_3.year$="2010." Thus, an authorship record r_i groups all citation attributes for each author name listed in a citation record.

Definition 2.3 (Ambiguous Group). An ambiguous group is a group of authorship records that includes ambiguous values for the attribute *authorname*, i.e., the authorship records in this group share similar author names.

Table 2.2: Examples of authorship records

Authorship Record	Attribute
r_1	$r_1.id$ = 1
	$r_1.author$ = S. Godbole
	$r_1.coauthor$ = I. Bhattacharya, A. Gupta, A. Verma
	$r_1.worktitle$ = Building re-usable dictionary repositories for real-world text mining
	$r_1.venuetitle$ = Proceedings of the 19th ACM International Conference on Information and Knowledge Management, CIKM 2010
	$r_1.publicationyear$ = 2010
r_2	$r_2.id$ = 1
	$r_2.author$ = I. Bhattacharya
	$r_2.coauthor$ = S. Godbole, A. Gupta, A. Verma
	$r_2.worktitle$ = Building re-usable dictionary repositories for real-world text mining
	$r_2.venuetitle$ = Proceedings of the 19th ACM International Conference on Information and Knowledge Management, CIKM 2010
	$r_2.publicationyear$ = 2010
r_3	$r_3.id$ = 1
	$r_3.author$ = A. Gupta
	$r_3.coauthor$ = S. Godbole, I. Bhattacharya, A. Verma
	$r_3.worktitle$ = Building re-usable dictionary repositories for real-world text mining
	$r_3.venuetitle$ = Proceedings of the 19th ACM International Conference on Information and Knowledge Management, CIKM 2010
	$r_3.publicationyear$ = 2010
r_4	$r_4.id$ = 1
	$r_4.author$ = A. Verma
	$r_4.coauthor$ = S. Godbole, I. Bhattacharya, A. Gupta
	$r_4.worktitle$ = Building re-usable dictionary repositories for real-world text mining
	$r_4.venuetitle$ = Proceedings of the 19th ACM International Conference on Information and Knowledge Management, CIKM 2010
	$r_4.publicationyear$ = 2010

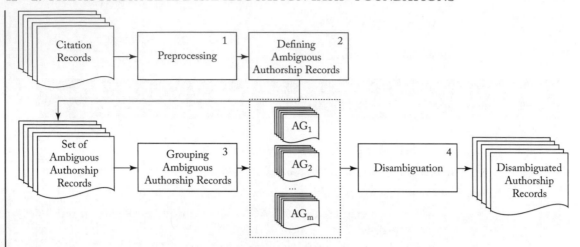

Figure 2.2: The author name disambiguation task.

2.2   THE AUTHOR NAME DISAMBIGUATION TASK

The author name disambiguation task may be formulated as follows. Let $C = \{c_1, c_2, \ldots, c_k\}$ be a set of citation records. Given a specific instance c_i of C, each value of its attribute *authornames* refers to a specific author and is associated with an authorship record r_j. Thus, an author name disambiguation method aims at producing a disambiguation function that is used to partition the set of authorship records $\{r_1, r_2, \ldots, r_m\}$ into n sets $\{a_1, a_2, \ldots, a_n\}$, so that each partition a_i contains (all and ideally only all) authorship records of a same author.

To better understand the disambiguation task, we split it in four steps, as illustrated in Figure 2.2: (1) Preprocessing; (2) Defining Ambiguous Authorship Records; (3) Grouping Ambiguous Authorship Records; and (4) Disambiguation. The Preprocessing step aims to prepare the citation records to the next steps. Usually, this includes a standardization of the author names, as well as the removal of stop-words and the stemming of work titles. Figure 2.3 shows the result of applying stop-word removal and stemming on the *worktitle* attribute of the citation record presented in Figure 2.1.

After preprocessing a citation record, Step 2 receives as input n authorship records, one for each of its author names. As mentioned before, we associate to each authorship record all attributes from a citation record but *authornames*, which we split into two other attributes: *authorname* (the author name associated with that authorship record) and *coauthorname*. Then, Step 3 (Grouping Ambiguous Authorship Records) splits the set of authorship records into ambiguous groups (authorship records whose author names are ambiguous). The ambiguous groups may be obtained, for instance, by using some blocking method [Backes, 2018, On et al., 2005]. Blocking methods address scalability issues, thus avoiding the need for comparing all

S. Godbole, I. Bhattacharya, A. Gupta, and A. Verma. (2010). build usabl dictionari repositori real world text mine. In *Proceedings of the 19th ACM International Conference on Information and Knowledge Management, CIKM 2010.* pages 1189–1198, Toronto, ON, Canada.

Figure 2.3: Example of a bibliographic reference after removing stop-words and stemming the work title.

authorship records. Finally, Step 4 applies a specific disambiguation method to each ambiguous group.

2.3 EVALUATION METRICS

In this section, we describe five metrics that are usually used for evaluating author name disambiguation methods. They are the K, pairwise F1, cluster F1, RCS, and B-Cubed metrics. The key idea is to compare the clusters generated by disambiguation methods against ideal, perfect clusters manually created [Kim, 2019]. As the methods should ideally group the records authored by the same author in a single cluster and separate those records belonging to different authors into distinct clusters, such metrics aim to measure the purity and cohesion of the clusters produced by them. In other words, these metrics estimate the number of authorship records belonging to the same author that are grouped into a specific cluster, as well as those that are split into several ones, thus indicating how related the records associated with a same author are. Hereafter, a cluster extracted by a disambiguation method will be referred to as an *empirical cluster*, while a perfect one will be referred to as a *theoretical cluster*.

2.3.1 THE K METRIC

The K metric determines the trade-off between the average cluster purity (ACP) and the average author purity (AAP). Given an ambiguous group, ACP evaluates the purity of the empirical clusters with respect to the theoretical ones for this ambiguous group. Thus, if the empirical clusters are pure (i.e., they contain only authorship records of the same author), the corresponding ACP value will be 1. ACP is given by Equation (2.1):

$$ \text{ACP} = \frac{1}{N} \sum_{i=1}^{e} \sum_{j=1}^{t} \frac{n_{ij}^2}{n_i}, \tag{2.1} $$

where N is the total number of authorship records in the ambiguous group, t is the number of theoretical clusters in the ambiguous group, e is the number of empirical clusters for this ambiguous group, n_{ij} is the total number of authorship records in the empirical cluster i that are also in the theoretical cluster j, and n_i is the total number of authorship records in the empirical cluster i.

Similarly, given an ambiguous group, the AAP metric evaluates the fragmentation of the empirical clusters with respect to the theoretical ones. If the empirical clusters are not fragmented, the corresponding AAP value will be 1. In other words, the AAP metric can be thought as the inverse of the fragmentation. The higher the AAP value is, the least fragmented the clusters are. AAP is given by Equation (2.2):

$$\text{AAP} = \frac{1}{N} \sum_{j=1}^{t} \sum_{i=1}^{e} \frac{n_{ij}^2}{n_j}, \tag{2.2}$$

where n_j is the total number of authorship records in the theoretical cluster j.

Finally, the K metric consists of the geometric mean between the ACP and AAP values. It evaluates the purity and fragmentation of the empirical clusters identified by a specific disambiguation method. The K metric is given by Equation (2.3):

$$K = \sqrt{\text{ACP} \times \text{AAP}}. \tag{2.3}$$

Although the above three metrics were proposed to a specific clustering task [Lapidot, 2002], due to their simplicity and effectivity they have been adopted for evaluating several author name disambiguation methods [Cota et al., 2010, de Carvalho et al., 2011, Ferreira et al., 2014, Pereira et al., 2009, Santana et al., 2017, Shin et al., 2014, Wu et al., 2014, Zhao et al., 2017].

2.3.2   PAIRWISE F1 AND CLUSTER F1

Pairwise F1 (pF1) is the F1 metric [Rijsbergen, 1979] calculated using pairwise precision and pairwise recall. Pairwise precision (pP) is calculated as $pP = \frac{a}{a+c}$, where a is the number of authorship record pairs in an empirical cluster that are (correctly) associated with the same author, whereas c is the number of authorship record pairs in an empirical cluster not corresponding to the same author. Pairwise recall (pR) is calculated as $pR = \frac{a}{a+b}$, where b is the number of authorship record pairs associated with the same author that are not in the same empirical cluster. Thus, the F1-metric is defined by Equation (2.4) as follows:

$$p\text{F1} = 2 \times \frac{pP \times pR}{pP + pR}. \tag{2.4}$$

Cluster F1 (cF1), on the other hand, is the F1 metric calculated using cluster precision and cluster recall, thus measuring the performance at the cluster level. Cluster precision (cP) is calculated as $cP = a/(a + c)$, where a is the number of correct clusters (a correct cluster should have all the authorship records of an author and only those, i.e., none from another author; otherwise it is incorrect) and c is the number of incorrect clusters. Cluster recall (cR) is calculated as $cR = a/(a + b)$, where b is the number of clusters that should be created but were not. This is a metric to summarize information about the correct clusters generated by the method. Thus, cF1 is analogously defined by Equation (2.5) as follows:

$$cF1 = 2 \times \frac{cP \times cR}{cP + cR}.$$ (2.5)

2.3.3   RATIO OF CLUSTER SIZE

The ratio of cluster size (RCS) is given by dividing the number of empirical clusters by the number of theoretical ones. This serves to evaluate how close is the measure to the ideal number of clusters to be generated.

2.3.4   B-CUBED

The B-Cubed metric was proposed by Bagga and Baldwin [1998] and has been used, for instance, to evaluate the Web person name search task [Artiles et al., 2010]. B-Cubed calculates the final precision and recall based on the precision (P_r) and recall (R_r) of each authorship record r, which are defined as:

$$P_r = \frac{n_i^r}{n_i}, \quad \text{and}$$ (2.6)

$$R_r = \frac{n_i^r}{n_j},$$ (2.7)

where n_i^r is the total number of authorship records that refer to the same author associated with r and belong to the a same empirical cluster i that contains r, n_i is the total number of authorship records in the empirical cluster i that contains r, and n_j is the total number of authorship records in the theoretical cluster j that contains r.

The final precision (bP) and recall (bR) are calculated by the following formulas:

$$bP = \sum_{r=1}^{N} w_r \times P_r, \quad \text{and}$$ (2.8)

$$bR = \sum_{r=1}^{N} w_r \times R_r,$$ (2.9)

where N is the number of authorship records in the collection and w_r is the weight of the authorship records r in the collection. The value of each w_r is commonly defined as $1/N$.

The harmonic mean (bF$_\alpha$) of B-Cubed precision and recall is calculated by:

$$bF_\alpha = \frac{1}{\alpha \frac{1}{bP} + (1 - \alpha)\frac{1}{bR}}.$$ (2.10)

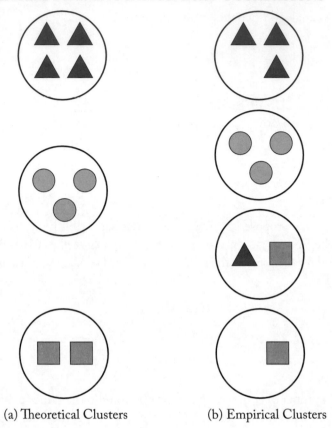

(a) Theoretical Clusters   (b) Empirical Clusters

Figure 2.4: An illustrative example. Each geometric figure corresponds to an authorship record that refers to an author. Equal geometric figures represent the same author.

2.3.5   APPLYING THE EVALUATION METRICS: AN ILLUSTRATIVE EXAMPLE

Consider the illustrative example shown in Figure 2.4, in which we have three theoretical clusters and four empirical ones. As we can see, in this example only one empirical cluster is not pure and there are two authorship records (represented by squares) that appear fragmented into two other clusters.

Table 2.3 shows the results of each metric applied to our illustrative example. To calculate the value of the ACP metric according to Equation (2.1), we must look at the empirical clusters. In the first cluster, we have three authorship records of the same author (three triangles), thus $n_{ij} = 3$ and $n_i = 3$, which yields the first fraction $\frac{3^2}{3}$ in the sum. In this fraction, the numerator indicates that we have three authorship records of the same author and the denominator indicates that we have three authorship records in the empirical cluster. In the second empirical cluster,

Table 2.3: Performance measured according to each evaluation metric

Metric	Calculation	Result
K	$ACP = \dfrac{1}{9} \times \left(\dfrac{3^2}{3} + \dfrac{3^2}{3} + \dfrac{1^2}{2} + \dfrac{1^2}{2} + \dfrac{1^2}{1} \right) = 0.89$ $AAP = \dfrac{1}{9} \times \left(\dfrac{3^2}{4} + \dfrac{3^2}{3} + \dfrac{1^2}{3} + \dfrac{1^2}{2} + \dfrac{1^2}{1} \right) = 0.73$	$K = 0.81$
pF1	$pP = \dfrac{3 + 3 + 0 + 0 + 0}{3 + 3 + 1 + 0} = 0.84$ $pR = \dfrac{3 + 3 + 0 + 0 + 0}{6 + 3 + 1} = 0.60$	$pF1 = 0.70$
B-Cubed	$bP = \dfrac{1}{9} \left(\dfrac{3}{3} + \dfrac{3}{3} + \dfrac{3}{3} + \dfrac{3}{3} + \dfrac{3}{3} + \dfrac{3}{3} + \dfrac{1}{2} + \dfrac{1}{2} + \dfrac{1}{1} \right) = 0.89$ $bR = \dfrac{1}{9} \left(\dfrac{3}{4} + \dfrac{3}{4} + \dfrac{3}{4} + \dfrac{3}{3} + \dfrac{3}{3} + \dfrac{3}{3} + \dfrac{1}{4} + \dfrac{1}{2} + \dfrac{1}{2} \right) = 0.72$	$bF_{\alpha=0.5} = 0.68$
cF1	$cP = \dfrac{1}{4} = 0.25$ $cR = \dfrac{1}{3} = 0.33$	$cF1 = 0.28$
RCS	$RCS = \dfrac{4}{3} = 1.33$	

we have the same situation, three authorship records of the same author (three circles) leading to the second term in the sum, $\frac{3^2}{3}$. The third empirical cluster has two authorship records of distinct authors leading to the two terms $\frac{1^2}{2}$. Finally, the last empirical cluster has a single authorship record that sums the term $\frac{1^2}{1}$. The final ACP result (0.89) is given by dividing the final sum by the total number of authorship records.

To calculate the value of the AAP metric, we also sum five fractions with the same numerators, but considering as denominators the number of authorship records in the corresponding theoretical clusters. For instance, the first fraction $\frac{3^2}{4}$ indicates three authorship records of the same author in the empirical cluster out of four in the theoretical one. The sum is also divided by nine, the total number of authorship records, leading to the AAP value of 0.73. Thus, the K value is the geometric mean of AAP and ACP, given by $\sqrt{0.89 \times 0.73} = 0.81$.

Pairwise F1, the harmonic mean of pairwise precision (pP) and recall (pR), is calculated according to the number of authorship record pairs in the theoretical and empirical clusters. In our illustrative example, the pP numerator sums three authorship record pairs of the same author in the first and second empirical clusters, and none in the last three ones. The denominator sums the total number of authorship record pairs from each empirical cluster. Thus, the final value of pP is 0.84. For calculating the value of the pR metric, we consider the same pP numerator, being the denominator the sum of the number of authorship record pairs that refer to the same author from the theoretical clusters: 6, 3, and 1 in the first, second, and third theoretical clusters, respectively. Thus, $pR = 0.60$ and $pF1 = 2 \times \frac{0.84 \times 0.60}{0.84 + 0.60} = 0.70$.

The B-cubed metric checks, in each empirical cluster, the number of authorship records of the same author of a given authorship record. For instance, in our example, to calculate bP, we sum $(\frac{3}{3} + \frac{3}{3} + \frac{3}{3} + \frac{3}{3} + \frac{3}{3} + \frac{3}{3} + \frac{1}{2} + \frac{1}{2} + \frac{1}{1})$, where the first three fractions $\frac{3}{3}$ correspond to the precision of each authorship record from the first empirical cluster (three authorship records of the same author out of three), the next three $\frac{3}{3}$ refer to the precision of the authorship records from the second empirical cluster, the two fractions $\frac{1}{2}$ (one out of two authorship records of the same author) consider the authorship records from the third empirical cluster, and the fraction $\frac{1}{1}$ is about the authorship record in the last empirical cluster.

To calculate bR for our example, the numerator of each fraction $\frac{n_i^r}{n_j}$ from the sum $(\frac{3}{4} + \frac{3}{4} + \frac{3}{4} + \frac{3}{3} + \frac{3}{3} + \frac{3}{3} + \frac{1}{4} + \frac{1}{2} + \frac{1}{2})$ indicates the number of authorship records in the empirical cluster i that is in the same theoretical cluster j of r divided by the number of authorship records in the theoretical cluster j. For instance, the first fraction $\frac{3}{4}$ indicates, for an authorship record from the first empirical cluster, that we have three out of four authorship records from the same theoretical cluster. We define $w_r = 1/9$ to weight the precision and recall of each one of the nine authorship records. Finally, we calculate the bF measure using $\alpha = 0.5$. Thus, $bF = 1/(0.5 \times \frac{1}{0.89} + (1 - \alpha) \times \frac{1}{0.72}) = 0.68$.

As we can see, ACP and AAP, components of the K metric, and bP and bR, components of the B-Cubed metric, produce similar results. On the other hand, pP and pR, components of $pF1$, show lower values compared to the aforementioned metrics, because they do not consider authorship records that cannot be paired with other ones from the same author in the same empirical cluster.

To calculate $cF1$, we consider the number of correct clusters, that is, the clusters with all and only all authorship records of an author. In our example, we have only one correct empirical cluster, the second one. Thus, $cP = 1/4$, i.e., one correct empirical cluster out of four, and $cR = 1/3$, i.e., one correct empirical cluster out of three theoretical ones. This leads to $cF1 = 2 \times \frac{0.25 \times 0.33}{0.25 + 0.33} = 0.28$, indicating few correct empirical clusters (only one in our example).

Finally, the RCS metric indicates the closeness of the number of theoretical and empirical clusters. In our example, RCS $= 4/3 = 1.33$ represents four empirical clusters against three theoretical ones. That is, the disambiguation method identified one author more than the actual ones.

2.4   FINAL COMMENTS

In this chapter, we provided a characterization of the author name disambiguation task. For this, we started by presenting some basic definitions, followed by a brief description of the main steps involved in this specific task. Then, we introduced some of the evaluation metrics most adopted in the literature and presented an illustrative example describing how they can be used to assess the performance of existing author name disambiguation methods.

CHAPTER 3

Taxonomy

Over the past years, several author name disambiguation methods have been proposed in the literature in the attempt to solve the author name ambiguity problem. To better understand the approaches followed by such methods, in this chapter we present a taxonomy that we have introduced to classify them according to the type of approach they adopt and the evidence they explore in the disambiguation task [Ferreira et al., 2012b].

We start by presenting an overview of our taxonomy for classifying author name disambiguation methods (Section 3.1). Then, we detail the classification of the methods according to the type of approach adopted (Section 3.2) and the kind of evidence explored by them (Section 3.3).

3.1 A TAXONOMY FOR AUTHOR NAME DISAMBIGUATION METHODS

Figure 3.1 shows our proposed taxonomy. Based on this taxonomy, existing methods may be initially classified into two distinct categories according to the main type of approach exploited by them: *author grouping* and *author assignment*.

Author grouping methods try to group the authorship records of a same author based on some type of similarity involving their attributes. Typical methods that follow this strategy are: CR – Collective Relational Entity Resolution [Bhattacharya and Getoor, 2007], HHC – Heuristic-based Hierarchical Clustering [Cota et al., 2010], LUCID – Author Name Disambiguation using Graph Structural Clustering [Hussain and Asghar, 2017a], FMC – Fast Multiple Clustering [Liu et al., 2015], WAD – Web Author Disambiguation [Pereira et al., 2009], NC – the Nearest Cluster method [Santana et al., 2015], GFAD – Graph Framework for Author Disambiguation [Shin et al., 2014], Author-ity – A model for author name disambiguation [Torvik et al., 2005, Torvik and Smalheiser, 2009], DSHAC – DST-based Hierarchical Agglomerative Clustering [Wu et al., 2014], NameClarifier [Shen et al., 2017], Disting [Peng et al., 2019] and those proposed by D'Angelo and van Eck [2020], Franzoni et al. [2018], Zhang et al. [2018], Kooli et al. [2018] and Müller [2017]. Notice that even methods that adopt very simple string matching strategies to address the author name disambiguation problem, such as those proposed by Backes [2018] and Milojevic [2013], should also be included in this category.

On the other hand, *author assignment* methods aim at directly assigning the authorship records to their respective authors by adopting either a *classification* technique or a *clustering* one. Typical examples of such methods are: INDi – Incremental Name Disambiguation [de Car-

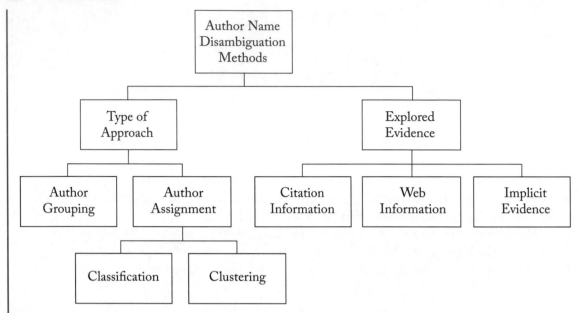

Figure 3.1: A taxonomy for author name disambiguation methods [Ferreira et al., 2012b].

valho et al., 2011], SAND – Self Training Author Name Disambiguation [Ferreira et al., 2014, 2010], Hierarchical Naive Bayes Mixture Model [Han et al., 2005a], INC – Incremental Nearest Cluster [Santana et al., 2017], SLAND – Self-training Lazy Associative Name Disambiguation [Veloso et al., 2012], HEEL – Exploratory Entity Linking for Heterogeneous Information Networks [Wang et al., 2020], and IFL – Incremental Learning Framework [Zhao et al., 2017].

Alternatively, the methods may be grouped according to the evidence explored in the disambiguation task, namely *citation attributes* (only), *Web information*, or *implicit data* that can be extracted from the available information (see the right-hand side branch of the taxonomy tree in Figure 3.1).

Notice that in this book we cover only automatic author name disambiguation methods. Other types of method, such as manual assignment by librarians [Scoville et al., 2003] or collaborative work,[1] rely heavily on human efforts, which prevent them from being used in massive author name disambiguation tasks. For this reason, they are not addressed here. There are also efforts to establish a unique identification to each author, such as the use of the Open Researcher and Contributor ID[2] (ORCID) [Haak et al., 2012], but these are also not covered here.

Since the name disambiguation problem is not restricted to a single context, it is also worth noticing that several other name disambiguation methods, which exploit distinct pieces of evidence or are targeted at other applications (e.g., name disambiguation in Web search results),

---

[1]http://meta.wikimedia.org/wiki/WikiAuthors
[2]http://www.orcid.org

have been described in the literature [Delgado et al., 2017, 2018, Diehl et al., 2006, On et al., 2014, Xu et al., 2015, Zhou et al., 2018]. However, a discussion of these methods is outside the scope of this book.

Finally, we should stress that the categories in our taxonomy are not completely disjoint. For instance, there are methods that use two or more types of evidence or mix approaches. In the next sections, we detail our proposed taxonomy.

3.2   TYPES OF APPROACH

As mentioned before, one way to categorize the several existing author name disambiguation methods is according to the type of approach they exploit. We elaborate this distinction further in the discussion below.

3.2.1   AUTHOR GROUPING METHODS

Author grouping methods apply a similarity function to the attributes of the authorship records (or groups of authorship records) in order to decide whether to group the corresponding authorship records using a clustering technique. The similarity function may be predefined (based on existing ones and depending on the type of the attribute) [Bhattacharya and Getoor, 2007, Cota et al., 2010, D'Angelo and van Eck, 2020, Han et al., 2005b, Liu et al., 2015, On and Lee, 2007, Shen et al., 2017, Soler, 2007, Wu et al., 2014, Zhang et al., 2019b, Zhu et al., 2018], learned using a supervised machine learning technique [Culotta et al., 2007, Huang et al., 2006, Kim et al., 2018, Louppe et al., 2016, Santana et al., 2015, Torvik et al., 2005, Torvik and Smalheiser, 2009, Tran et al., 2014, Treeratpituk and Lee Giles, 2009], or extracted from the relationships among authors and coauthors, usually represented by a graph [Fan et al., 2011, Franzoni et al., 2018, Hussain and Asghar, 2017a, Levin and Heuser, 2010, Ma et al., 2019, On et al., 2006, Shin et al., 2014, Zhang and Al Hasan, 2017].

The defined similarity function is then used along with some clustering technique to group authorship records of a same author, trying to maximize intra-cluster similarities and minimize inter-cluster ones, respectively.

Figures 3.2 and 3.3 present an example that illustrates the general functioning of an author grouping method. Figure 3.2 shows five citation records with ambiguous author names, "Mohammed J. Zaki," "Mohammed Zaki," and "M. Zaki," which may refer either to the same author or to different ones. An author grouping method works by comparing each record to the other ones to decide whether they correspond to the same author or not. In this example, we notice that two of the three blue records share at least another common coautor name ("P. Anchuri"). In addition, all these records refer to a publication related to some topic on data mining or knowledge discovery. Such features may be used by a grouping method to consider these three records as belonging to the same author. Differently, the other two records do not share exact coauthor names, but they are related to Network Security and were published in the same journal, thus indicating they may belong to the same author. An author grouping method

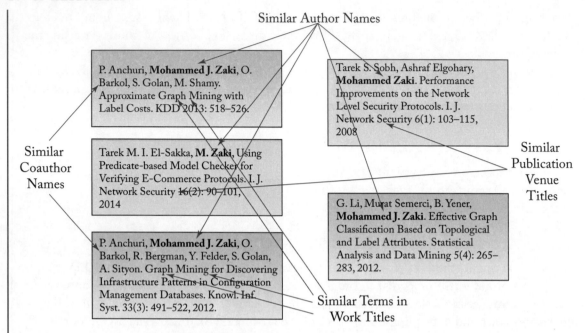

Figure 3.2: Example of author grouping: pieces of evidence considered.

checks the similarity between the records based on their attributes, in order to assign to the same cluster those belonging to the same author. For our example, the result is the one shown in Figure 3.3 with two clusters, the first belonging to Mohammed Javeed Zaki from the Rensselaer Polythechnic Institute and the second belonging to Mohammed Zaki from the Al-Azhar University.

Strategies for Defining a Similarity Function

A similarity function is responsible for determining how similar two authorship records (or groups of authorship records) are. The goal is to define a function that returns high similarity values for authorship records of the same author and low similarity values for authorship records of different authors. Moreover, this similarity function should be transitive. More specifically, being c_1, c_2, and c_3 three citation records, if c_1 and c_2 are very similar according to a function f, and c_2 and c_3 are also very similar according to the same function f, then c_1 and c_3 should also be very similar to each other according to f. Next, we briefly discuss some strategies to define such a kind of similarity function.

Using Predefined Functions.   This class of methods has a specific predefined similarity function S embedded in their algorithms to check whether two authorship records or groups of authorship records refer to the same author. Examples of such a function S include [Cohen

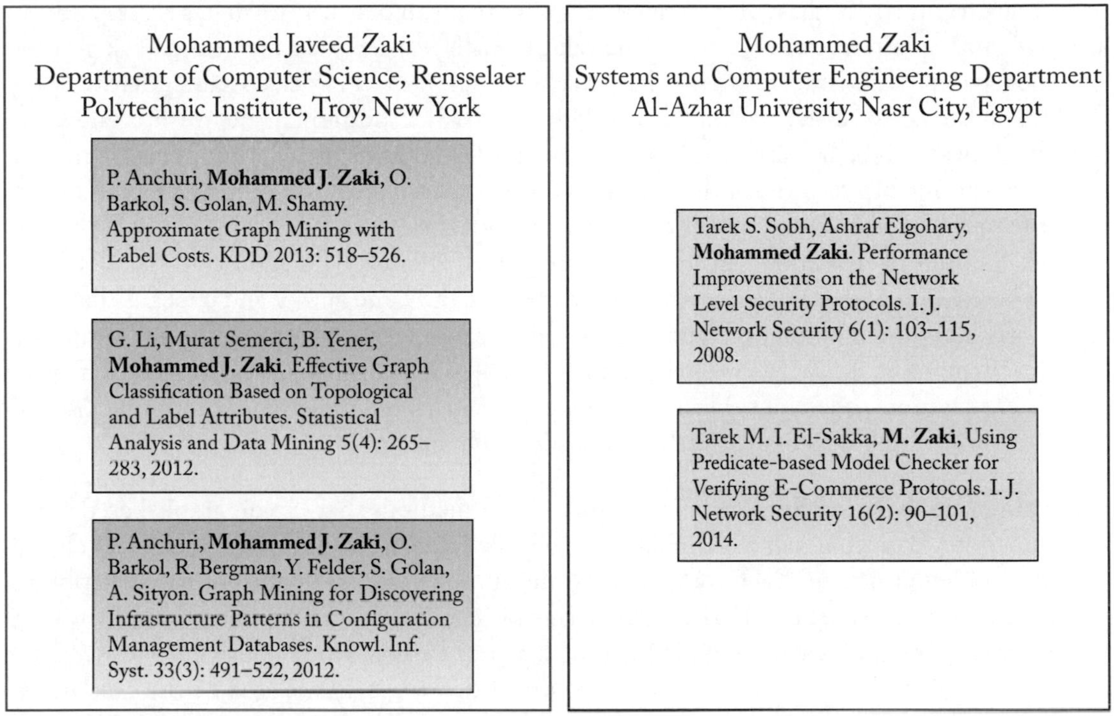

Mohammed Javeed Zaki
Department of Computer Science, Rensselaer
Polytechnic Institute, Troy, New York

Mohammed Zaki
Systems and Computer Engineering Department
Al-Azhar University, Nasr City, Egypt

P. Anchuri, **Mohammed J. Zaki**, O. Barkol, S. Golan, M. Shamy. Approximate Graph Mining with Label Costs. KDD 2013: 518–526.

G. Li, Murat Semerci, B. Yener, **Mohammed J. Zaki**. Effective Graph Classification Based on Topological and Label Attributes. Statistical Analysis and Data Mining 5(4): 265–283, 2012.

P. Anchuri, **Mohammed J. Zaki**, O. Barkol, R. Bergman, Y. Felder, S. Golan, A. Sityon. Graph Mining for Discovering Infrastructure Patterns in Configuration Management Databases. Knowl. Inf. Syst. 33(3): 491–522, 2012.

Tarek S. Sobh, Ashraf Elgohary, **Mohammed Zaki**. Performance Improvements on the Network Level Security Protocols. I. J. Network Security 6(1): 103–115, 2008.

Tarek M. I. El-Sakka, **M. Zaki**, Using Predicate-based Model Checker for Verifying E-Commerce Protocols. I. J. Network Security 16(2): 90–101, 2014.

Figure 3.3: Example of author grouping: final result.

et al., 2003]: the Levenshtein distance, Jaccard coefficient, cosine similarity, and soft-TFIDF, among others that might be applied to specific attributes of an authorship record, like the Fragment Comparison Function [Oliveira, 2005] described in Appendix A. Ad-hoc combinations of such functions have also been used in some methods [Bhattacharya and Getoor, 2007, Liu et al., 2015, Shen et al., 2017, Soler, 2007]. These methods do not need any type of supervision in terms of training data, but their similarity functions are usually tuned to disambiguate a specific collection of citation records. For different collections, a new tuning procedure may be required. Finally, it is important to notice that not all the functions used by these methods are transitive by nature.

Learning a Similarity Function.   Learning a specific similarity function usually produces better results, since these learned functions are directly optimized for the disambiguation problem at hand. To learn a similarity function, the disambiguation methods receive a set $\{s_{ij}\}$ of pairs of authorship records (the training data) along with a special variable that informs whether these two corresponding authorship records refer to the same author. The pair of authorship records, r_i and $r_j \in R$ (the set of authorship records) are usually represented by a similarity vector $\vec{s}_{ij}$. Each similarity vector $\vec{s}_{ij}$ is composed of a set $\mathcal{F}$ of q features $\{f_1, f_2, \ldots, f_q\}$.

Each feature f_p of these vectors represents a comparison between attributes $r_i \cdot A_l$ and $r_j \cdot A_l$ of two authorship records, r_i and r_j. The value of each feature is usually defined using other functions such as Levenshtein distance, Jaccard coefficient, Jaro-Winkler, cosine similarity, soft-TFIDF, or Euclidean distance [Gomaa and Fahmy, 2013]. Additionaly, the feature value can be defined by a specific heuristic such as the number of title terms or coauthor names common to the two authorship records, or the distance between special strings that might represent the author names (e.g., first name initials concatenated with the last name).

A training data is then carried out to produce a similarity function S from $R \times R$ to $\{0, 1\}$, where 1 means that the authorship records refer to the same author and 0 means that they do not. As mentioned before, methods relying on learning techniques to define the similarity function [Santana et al., 2015, Smalheiser and Torvik, 2009, Tran et al., 2014] are quite effective in different citation collections, but they usually need many examples and a minimum set of features to work well, which are usually very costly to obtain.

Exploiting Graph-based Similarity Functions.   The methods that exploit graph-based similarity functions for author name disambiguation usually create a coauthorship graph $G = (V, E)$ for each ambiguous group. Each component of the author name and coauthor name attributes is represented by a vertex $v \in V$. The same coauthor names are usually represented by only a unique vertex. Then, for each coauthorship (i.e., a pair of authors who publish a work together) an edge $\langle v_i, v_j \rangle \in E$ is created. The weight of each edge $\langle v_i, v_j \rangle$ is related to the amount of articles coauthored by the corresponding author names represented by vertices v_i and v_j. A graph-based metric (e.g., shortest path as adopted by Levin and Heuser [2010]) may be combined with other similarity functions on the attributes of the authorship records or used as a new feature in the similarity vectors.

Clustering Techniques

Author grouping methods usually exploit a clustering technique in their disambiguation task. The most used techniques are partitioning, hierarchical agglomerative clustering, density-based and spectral clustering [Han et al., 2011, Zaki and Meira Jr, 2014]. In general, these clustering techniques rely on a "good similarity function" to group the authorship records. Next, we provide a brief description of these techniques applied to the author name ambiguity problem.

Partitioning Clustering.   A partitioning clustering technique, applied to the author name ambiguity problem [Kanani et al., 2007, Yang et al., 2008], creates k partitions of the set of authorship records. These methods usually receive the number k of author groups to be created as input as well as the set of authorship records to be disambiguated. They create an initial partitioning of k clusters (usually randomly) and, to improve the disambiguation process, move authorship records from one cluster to another based on some similarity criteria. The aim is that, in the end of the process, the authorship records of a same author will be put together in the same cluster while authorship records of different authors will remain in different clusters.

One advantage of these partitioning techniques is that an authorship record may be assigned to different authors during the disambiguation process, which can potentially help reducing erroneous assignments. This does not occur in hierarchical agglomerative clustering techniques (see below). However, these methods usually need to know the correct number of authors to perform well, which in most of cases is an unrealistic assumption. Moreover, similarities are usually calculated with respect to a representative authorship record within the clusters (e.g., a centroid). Thus, authorship records that are not similar enough to this representative one but are similar to other authorship records in the cluster may not be inserted into this (perhaps correct) cluster.

Hierarchical Agglomerative Clustering.   A hierarchical agglomerative clustering technique [Han et al., 2011, Zaki and Meira Jr, 2014] groups the authorship records in a hierarchical manner. Initially, each authorship record corresponds to a single cluster. Next, in each iteration of the process, the two most similar clusters are grouped together and the similarity among all clusters is recalculated [Liu et al., 2015, Santana et al., 2015, Wu et al., 2014, Zhang et al., 2018]. The process finishes when there is only a single cluster fusing all others or the similarity between the clusters reaches a given threshold.

One disadvantage of this technique is that if two authorship records of different authors are put together in a same cluster during the process, they can no longer be moved to another cluster for the remainder of the process, i.e., this type of error cannot be corrected. In the case of the name disambiguation task, this particular homonym problem is one of the hardest to correct. An other disadvantage is the cost: we usually need to compare all clusters with each other to find the most suitable to be fused.

Density-based Clustering.   When applying a density-based clustering method, a cluster corresponds to a dense region of authorship records surrounded by a region of low density (according to some density criteria). Authorship records in regions with low density are considered as noise.

An example of a density-based clustering algorithm that has been used in the author name disambiguation task [Huang et al., 2006, Kim et al., 2016] is DBSCAN [Han et al., 2011, Zaki and Meira Jr, 2014]. DBSCAN estimates the density of authorship records by counting the number of authorship records within a specified radius. It classifies each authorship record as either a core authorship record (i.e., an authorship record whose number of neighbors within a specific radius exceeds a given threshold), a border authorship record (i.e., an authorship record that is not a core one, but is within the neighborhood of a core authorship record) or a noise authorship record (i.e., an authorship record that is neither core nor border).

DBSCAN initially labels all authorship records as core, border or noise based on the procedure described above. Next, it disconsiders all noise authorship records and introduces edges between the core authorship records within a given radius of each other. Each group of connected authorship records is a cluster and each border authorship record is associated with one cluster of its core authorship records.

One advantage of density-based clustering techniques is that the clusters are constructed using several representative authorship records. A disadvantage is that they are very sensible to their thresholds.

Spectral Clustering.   Spectral clustering techniques [Zha et al., 2001] are graph-based techniques that compute the eigenvalues and eigenvectors, the spectral information, of a Laplacian Matrix that, in the author name disambiguation task, represents a similarity matrix of a weighted graph $G = (V, E)$. In this way, each vertex $v \in V$ represents an authorship record and each weighted edge $\langle v_i, v_j \rangle$ represents the similarity between the attributes of the vertices v_i and v_j. A graph-based technique splits the vertices into clusters by maximizing the weights of intra-cluster vertices and minimizing the weights of the inter-clusters vertices. A spectral clustering technique uses the spectral information (i.e., eigenvalues and eigenvectors) instead of the similarity matrix in the clustering process.

Spectral clustering usually produces better performance than traditional clustering techniques. However, the spectral clustering method used by Han et al. [2005b] for author name disambiguation needs to know the correct number of authors (clusters), which, as discussed before, can be unrealistic in real scenarios.

Graph-based Clustering.   Graph-based clustering techniques aim to find subgraphs (i.e., clusters), such that the vertices within these subgraphs are well connected, whereas vertices in other subgraphs are connected in a much weaker way [Han et al., 2011, Zaki and Meira Jr, 2014]. In the author name disambiguation task, graph-based methods [Hussain and Asghar, 2017a, Shin et al., 2014] usually construct a coauthorship graph $G = (V, E)$, where each vertex $v \in V$ represents an author and each edge $\{e_i, e_j\} \in E$ represents a coauthorship between the authors represented by the vertices e_i and e_j. Thus, such methods try to find out communities in G (i.e., well connected subgraphs) and hubs (i.e., vertices connecting such communities). A hub may indicate a homonym problem and, according to the number of communities bridged by it, a graph-based disambiguation method may split such a vertex to solve this problem.

3.2.2   AUTHOR ASSIGNMENT METHODS

Author assignment methods directly assign each authorship record by constructing a model that represents the author (for instance, the probabilities of an author publishing an article with other (co-)authors, in a given publication venue and using a list of specific terms in the work title) using either a supervised classification technique [Ferreira et al., 2010, Han et al., 2004, Wang et al., 2020, Zhao et al., 2017] or a model-based clustering one [Bhattacharya and Getoor, 2006, Han et al., 2005a].

To illustrate the approach followed by the author assignment methods, let us consider the example shown in Figures 3.4 and 3.5. Initially, in Figure 3.4, there exist two authors represented by the same name, "Jim Smith." The first author, referred to as Author A, is a professor at Department of Statistics of the University of Warwick. The second one, referred to as Author

Author A
Professor Jim Smith
Department of Statistics, University of Warwick
Publications
S. Liverani, P.E. Anderson, K.D. Edwards, A.J. Millar, and **J. Smith**. (2009) "Efficient Utility-based Clustering over High Dimensional Partition Spaces" J. of Bayesian Analysis, Vol. 04, No. 03, 539–572
J. Smith, P.E. Anderson, and S. Liverani. (2008) "Separation Measures and the Geometry of Bayes factor selection for Classification" J. Roy. Statist. Soc. B, Vol. 70, Part 5, 957–980
...

Author B
Professor Jim Smith
Faculty of Environment and Technology, The University of the West of England
Publications
J. Smith. The Co-Evolution of Memetic Algorithms for Protein Structure Prediction. In W.E. Hart, N. Krasnogor, and J.E. Smith, editors, *Recent Advances in Memetic Algorithms*, pp. 105–128, Springer, Berlin, Heidelberg, New York, 2004
N. Krasnogor and **J. Smith**. "A tutorial for Competent Memetic Algorithms: Model, Taxonomy, and Design Issues. *IEEE Transactions on Evolutionary Computation*, 9(5): 474–488, 2005.
...

Figure 3.4: Example of author assignment: existing authorship records.

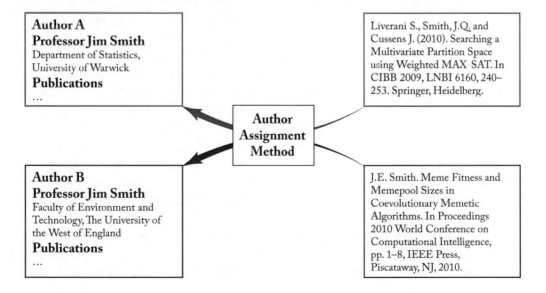

Figure 3.5: Example of author assignment: new citation records.

B, is a professor at Faculty of Environment and Technology of The University of the West of England. Each one of them has a list of previous publications. An author assignment method uses such a list to learn a function/model to represent the authors. When a new authorship record needs to be disambiguated, an author assignment method will assign this record to the correct author, using the learned function.

Looking at Figure 3.5, we can see two new citation records. The first one includes the author name "J. Q. Smith" and the second one the author name "J. E. Smith." The author assignment method receives the first authorship record and, using its attributes' values and the learned assignment function, infers Author A as its author. For this, it takes into consideration the current list of publications of Author A (see Figure 3.4). The blue arrow in Figure 3.5 indicates this assignment. Notice that the first authorship record and Author A share a same coauthor name ("S. Liverani"). The second authorship record follows a similar process, but it is assigned to Author B as indicated by the red arrow. This assignment occurs due to the similarity between the work title in the authorship record and the titles of Author B's publications as identified by the learned assignment function due to the existence of some common terms between them ("Co-Evolution" and "Memetic Algorithms").

Methods Based on Classification Techniques

Methods in this class assign the authorship records to their authors using a supervised machine learning technique. More specifically, they receive as input a set of authorship records with their respective attributes, i.e., the *training data* (denoted as $\mathcal{D}$), which consists of examples, in this case authorship records for which the correct author is known. Each example is composed of a set $\mathcal{F}$ of m features $\{f_1, f_2, \ldots, f_m\}$ along with a special variable called the *author*. This *author* variable draws its value from a discrete set of labels $\{a_1, a_2, \ldots, a_n\}$, in which each label uniquely identifies an author. The training examples are used to produce a disambiguation function (i.e., the disambiguator) that relates the features in the training examples to the correct author. The *test set* (denoted as $\mathcal{T}$) for the disambiguation task consists of a set of authorship records for which the features are known while the correct author is unknown. The disambiguator, which is a function from $\{f_1, f_2, \ldots, f_m\}$ to $\{a_1, a_2, \ldots, a_n\}$, is used to predict the correct author for the authorship records in the test set. In this context, the disambiguator essentially divides the records in $\mathcal{T}$ into n sets $\{a_1, a_2, \ldots, a_n\}$, where a_i contains (ideally all and no other) authorship records in which the ith author is included.

These methods are usually very effective when faced with a large number of examples of citations for each author. Another advantage is that, if the collection has been disambiguated (manually or automatically), the methods may be applied only to authorship records of the new citations inserted into the collection by simply running the learned model on them. Although successful cases of applying such methods have been reported in the literature [Ferreira et al., 2012b, Hussain and Asghar, 2017b], the acquisition of training examples usually requires skilled human annotators to manually label authorship records. Bibliographic repositories are very dynamic systems, thus manual labeling of large volumes of examples is unfeasible, requiring effective sampling strategies [Ferreira et al., 2012c]. Further, the disambiguation task presents nuances that impose the need for methods with specific abilities. For instance, since it is not reasonable to assume that examples for all possible authors are included in the training data and considering that the authors change their interests over time, new examples need to be inserted into training data continuously and the methods need to be retrained periodically in order to maintain their effectiveness.

Methods Based on Clustering Techniques

Clustering techniques [Han et al., 2011] attempt to directly assign authorship records to authors' works by optimizing the fit between a set of authorship records and some mathematical model used to represent that author. They use probabilistic techniques to determine the author in a iterative way to fit the model (or estimate the parameters in probabilistic techniques) of the authors. For instance, in the first run of such a method each authorship record may be randomly distributed to an author a_i and a function, from a set of features $\{f_1, f_2, \ldots, f_m\}$ to $\{a_1, a_2, \ldots, a_n\}$, is derived using this distribution. In the second iteration, this function is used to predict the author of each authorship record and a new function is derived to be used in the next iteration. This process continues until a stop condition is reached, for instance, after a number of iterations. Two algorithms commonly used to fit the models in disambiguation tasks are Expectation-Maximization [Dempster et al., 1977] and Gibbs Sampling [Griffiths and Steyvers, 2004].

These methods need no training examples, but usually require privileged information about the correct number of authors or the number of author groups (i.e., group of authors that publish together) and may take some time to estimate their parameters due, due to their iterative nature. Additionally, these methods may be able to directly assign authors to their authorship records in new citations using the final derived function.

3.3 EXPLORED EVIDENCE

In this section, we describe the kinds of evidence most commonly explored by the author name disambiguation methods, namely *citation information*, *Web information*, and *implicit evidence*.

Citation information comprises attributes directly extracted from citation records, such as author and coauthor names, work title, publication venue title, publication year, and so on. These attributes are the ones used by most author name disambiguation methods described in the literature, since they are commonly found in all citation records, but usually are not sufficient to perfectly disambiguate all authorship records of a specific author name. Some methods also assume the availability of additional information, such as e-mail addresses, postal addresses, webpage headers, text, etc. [Han et al., 2017, Huang et al., 2006, Soler, 2007, Torvik and Smalheiser, 2009, Treeratpituk and Lee Giles, 2009, Wu et al., 2014], which are not always available or easy to obtain, although, if existent, they usually help the disambiguation process.

Web information represents data retrieved from the Web that is used as additional information about an author's publication profile. This kind of information is usually obtained by submitting queries to search engines based on the values of citation attributes and the returned web pages are used as new evidence (attributes) to calculate the similarity among authorship records [Abdulhayoglu and Thijs, 2017, Kanani et al., 2007, Kang et al., 2009, Mondal and Chandra, 2020, Pereira et al., 2009, Wang et al., 2020, Yang et al., 2008]. The new evidence usually improves the disambiguation task. A major problem with this strategy is the additional cost for extracting all the needed information from the web pages.

Finally, implicit evidence is inferred from visible elements of attributes. Several techniques have been implemented to find implicit evidence, such as the latent topics of a citation. One example is the Latent Direchlet Location (LDA) [Blei et al., 2003] that estimates the topic distribution of a citation (i.e., LDA estimates the probability of each topic given a citation). This estimated distribution is used as new evidence (attribute) to calculate the similarity among authorship records [Shu et al., 2009, Song et al., 2007].

3.4   FINAL COMMENTS

In this chapter, we presented a taxonomy that we introduced in a previous work [Ferreira et al., 2012b] to classify existing author name disambiguation methods. According to our proposed taxonomy, author name disambiguation methods can be roughly classified from two specific perspectives, the type of approach they adopt and the evidence they explore to carry out the task at hand. Thus, based on this taxonomy, we then classified some of the most relevant methods proposed in the literature, providing a framework to better understand their main aspects.

CHAPTER 4

Heuristic-Based Hierarchical Clustering Disambiguation

With Ricardo G. Cota

The Heuristic-based Hierarchical Clustering (HHC) [Cota et al., 2010] is a simple, but effective, author grouping method that attempts to solve the author name disambiguation problem based on the following two real-world assumptions: (i) very rarely two authors with similar names and sharing a coauthor in common would be two distinct persons in the real world; and (ii) authors tend to publish on the same subjects and in the same venues for some portion of their careers. HHC follows these two assumptions to group the authorship records belonging to a same author.

In this chapter, we first provide an overview of HHC (Section 4.1) and then describe its two processing steps (Sections 4.2 and 4.3). Thus, according to our taxonomy introduced in Chapter 3, HHC is an typical example of an author grouping method that groups the authorship records in a hierarchical manner, assessing their similarity by means of a predefined function, exploiting only citation information as evidence.

4.1 OVERVIEW OF HHC

HHC deals at the same time with the *Mixed Citation* (MC) and *Split Citation* (SC) problems by combining similarity functions with application-oriented heuristics that use evidence present in the authorship records of authors we want to disambiguate. By considering as candidates for clustering in its first step only authorship records of authors with similar names (i.e., authors whose names have some similarity according to some matching function) and forcing them to have at least one "similar" coauthor in common, HHC deals with the MC problem, i.e., it diminishes the chances that the publication of two different authors will be mixed in the same group. On the other hand, by relying on other similarity evidence (but still considering similar names) based on the intuition that the publications of an author share some similar features (e.g., they have a common coauthor or address the same subject) to decide whether existing groups should be fused, HHC deals with the SC problem, i.e., it joins together groups that should not be separated. At the same time, authorship records from groups that do not share any similar features are not clustered together, thus diminishing the chances of mixing publications

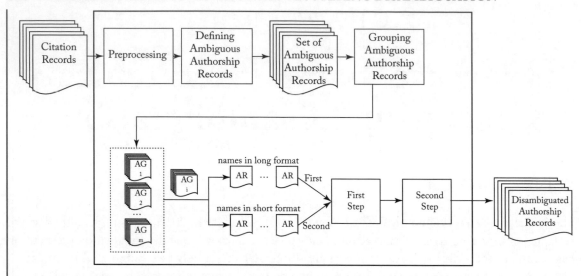

Figure 4.1: HHC overview.

of different authors. Notice that solving these two problems at the same time is hard since these two goals are in some sense conflicting and a good solution should find the proper balance.

HHC addresses the name disambiguation problem in two main steps after a preprocessing phase that treats the authorship records by removing stop-words and stemming the words appearing in the titles of the works and publication venues.[1] It first creates the authorship records and then groups those that include ambiguous author names (see Figure 4.1). Hereafter, we refer to these groups as *ambiguous groups*.

Algorithm 4.1 describes HHC. It receives as input a list R of authorship records and returns a list C of clusters of such records. Lines 5–7 of Algorithm 1 correspond to the preprocessing phase. To obtain the list G of ambiguous groups, any blocking strategy (see the work by On et al. [2005] for specific strategies) may be used, since the main aim here is to reduce the complexity of the problem. Thus, fusing only clusters with similar names considerably diminishes the number of possible comparisons. After producing the list G of ambiguous groups, for each ambiguous group g in G, HHC applies its two main steps (Lines 10 and 11) to generate the list of authorship record clusters (Line 12).

4.2 HHC FIRST STEP

Algorithm 4.2 describes the first HHC step. We will refer to Figure 4.2 when discussing it. This algorithm receives an ambiguous group g and returns a list C of clusters of authorship

---

[1]The original implementation of HHC uses the Porter's algorithm [Porter, 1980] for stemming the titles of the works and publication venues.

Algorithm 4.1 HHC

Require: List R of citation records;
Ensure: List C of clusters of authorship records;

1: Let A be a list of authorship records;
2: Let C_1 and C_2 be lists of clusters;
3: Let G be a list of ambiguous groups;
4: Let R' be a list of citation records;
5: $R' \leftarrow$ PreprocessCitationRecords(R);
6: $A \leftarrow$ CreateAuthorshipRecords(R');
7: $G \leftarrow$ CreateAmbiguousGroups(A);
8: $C \leftarrow \emptyset$
9: **for each** ambiguous group g in G **do**
10:    $C_1 \leftarrow$ FirstStep(g);
11:    $C_2 \leftarrow$ SecondStep(C_1);
12:    $C \leftarrow C \cup C_2$;
13: **end for**

Algorithm 4.2 FirstStep

Require: Ambiguous group g;
Ensure: List C of clusters of authorship records;

1: Let L and S be lists of authorship records;
2: Let C, C_1 and C_2 be lists of clusters;
3: $S \leftarrow$ GetShortNameRecords(g);
4: $L \leftarrow$ GetLongNameRecords(g);
5: $C_1 \leftarrow \emptyset$;
6: $C_2 \leftarrow$ ProcessList(L,C_1);
7: $C \leftarrow$ ProcessList(S,C_2);

---

records. It processes g by splitting it into two separate lists: S with records whose author names occur in a short format (see Figure 4.2a) and L with the remaining ones (i.e., those authorship records whose ambiguous author names are not in a short format). Then, it proceeds by first processing list L (Line 6) and then list S (Line 7). When processing lists L and S, the initial clusters of authorship records are built using the author name and the list of coauthor names as evidence. The idea of first processing the list of long names is that these names provide more evidence for our similarity functions to decide whether two authors have similar names or not. Figure 4.2b illustrates the HHC first step when applied to a sample list of authorship records S containing only short names. Note that the second and the third authorship records have been

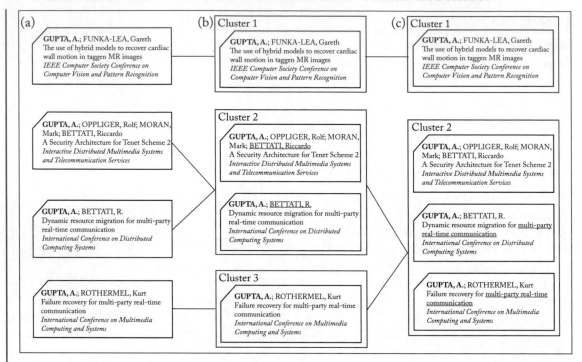

Figure 4.2: (a) Initial list of authorship records. (b) Clusters generated by the HHC first step. (c) Final result after the fusion phase.

clustered together because they have in common a similar coauthor name ("Riccardo Bettati" and "Bettati, R."). This strategy is based on a general heuristic that assumes that very rarely two authors with similar names that share a common coauthor would be two different persons in the real world. As shown by our experimental results [Cota et al., 2010], this heuristic proved to be very effective when applied to our method. This process generates very pure (i.e., with few wrong records within a cluster) but very fragmented (i.e., many records related to a same author are spread in different clusters) sets of clusters.

Algorithm 4.3 describes the function ProcessList used to process the list of authorship records in Algorithm 4.2 (Lines 6 and 7). This function receives a list A of authorship records and a list C_i of clusters of authorship records, and then returns a new list C_o with each authorship record a from A in some cluster c of C_o. Then, it compares the author name from each authorship record a with the author name from the first authorship record within each cluster c. If the author name from a is similar to the author name from the first authorship record of c and exists a coauthor name in a that is similar to some coauthor name in c, a is inserted in this cluster c (Line 7); otherwise, a new cluster is created with this authorship record a (Line 13).

Algorithm 4.3 ProcessList function

Require: List A of authorship records;
Require: List C_i of authorship record clusters;
Ensure: List C_o of authorship record clusters;

```
 1: C_o ← C_i;
 2: for each a in A do
 3:     inserted ← false;
 4:     c ← first(C_o);
 5:     while not inserted and c ≠ null do
 6:         if the author name from a is similar with the author name from the first authorship
            record of c and exists a coauthor name in a that is similar with some coauthor name in
            c then
 7:             InsertAuthorshipRecord(a, c);
 8:             inserted ←true;
 9:         end if
10:         c ← next(C_o);
11:     end while
12:     if inserted = false then
13:         c ← CreateNewCluster(a);
14:         Append(C_o, c);
15:     end if
16: end for
```

4.3   HHC SECOND STEP

Algorithm 4.4 describes the second step of HHC. This step aims at reducing fragmentation by using additional information from the authorship records when processing the initial clusters[2] in order to fuse them. This step is based on the general heuristic that presupposes that authors tend to publish on the same subjects and in the same venues for some portion of their careers. Thus, in the second step, HHC then proceeds in a hierarchical manner and fuses the clusters created in the first step based on their contents. Clusters are pairwise compared (Line 12) and, to determine whether two clusters can be fused, it estimates their similarity based on the words that compose the work and publication venue titles of their respective citations, if the names of the authors in the clusters are similar. If the estimated similarity of the words that compose either these attributes is higher than a given threshold, the two clusters are fused (Lines 12–16). This process continues until the termination criterion is met, i.e., until no more clusters can be fused. The final result is a list C_o of clusters with their respective authorship records (Figure 4.2c

---

[2]In its original implementation [Cota et al., 2010], HHC used only work and publication venue titles when executing this step. However, other attributes of a citation record, like the publication year, might be used for better matching.

Algorithm 4.4 SecondStep

Require: List C_i of clusters of authorship records;
Ensure: List C_o of clusters of authorship records;

1: $C_o \leftarrow C_i$;
2: $fused \leftarrow$ **true**;
3: **while** $fused$ **do**
4:    $fused \leftarrow$ **false**;
5:   **for each** c_1 in C_o **do**
6:     **for each** c_2 in C_o **do**
7:       **if** $c_1 \neq c_2$ **and** the first author name from c_1 is similar with the first author name from c_2 **then**
8:         $t_{t1} \leftarrow$ GetWorkTitleTerms(c_1);
9:         $t_{t2} \leftarrow$ GetWorkTitleTerms(c_2);
10:        $t_{v1} \leftarrow$ GetPublicationVenueTitleTerms(c_1);
11:        $t_{v2} \leftarrow$ GetPublicationVenueTitleTerms(c_2);
12:        **if** TitleSimilarity$(t_{t1}, t_{t2}) >$ title-threshold **or** VenueSimilarity$(t_{v1}, t_{v2}) >$ venue-threshold **then**
13:          $c_1 \leftarrow$ Fuse(c_1, c_2);
14:          remove(C_o, c_2);
15:          $fused \leftarrow$ **true**;
16:        **end if**
17:       **end if**
18:     **end for**
19:   **end for**
20: **end while**

---

in our running example). In this particular example, Clusters 2 and 3 in Figure 4.2b were fused into Cluster 2 in Figure 4.2c based on the similarity of their venue titles.

Notice that each time two or more clusters of "similar" authors are fused, the resulting cluster becomes "information richer," since the information of fused clusters is aggregated to it (e.g., all words in the publication titles are considered together). This provides more information for the next round of fusion, thus helping to increase the similarity among clusters, which is recomputed after each fusing iteration.

4.4 FINAL COMMENTS

Different similarity functions can be used for each kind of attribute of an authorship record. In its original implementation [Cota et al., 2010], for author and coauthor names, HHC used a function derived from the Fragment Comparison function [Oliveira, 2005], an edit-distance matching function specially designed for persons' names,[3] whereas for work and publication venue titles it used the cosine similarity function [Salton et al., 1975]. We notice that, in the worst case, the computational complexity of HHC is $\mathcal{O}(n^2)$, where n is the total number of authorship records to be disambiguated. However, since the similarity functions are usually applied on small strings, they are not affected by the collection size.

In our experimental evaluation [Cota et al., 2010], using the Cota-DBLP and Cota-BDBComp datasets described in Appendix C, HHC was compared with four author name disambiguation methods: two supervised author assignment methods (based on the Naïve Bayes and Support Vector Machine (SVM) techniques) [Han et al., 2004], a supervised author grouping method (based on the SVM and DBScan techniques) [Huang et al., 2006], and an unsupervised grouping method based on the K-way spectral clustering technique [Han et al., 2005b]. Experimental results demonstrated the superiority of HHC over all baselines but the supervised SVM-based method in the Cota-DBLP dataset when considering the K metric, and the method based on the k-way spectral clustering technique, with which HHC statistically tied in the Cota-BDBComp dataset, when considering both, the K and pF1 metrics. Remember that, unlike the SVM-based method and the K-way spectral clustering technique, HHC requires no training data and does not make use of any privileged information such as the number of correct groups to be generated, which are advantages from a practical viewpoint.

Finally, the good performance of HHC can be attributed to its simple heuristics, which consider that very rarely two authors with similar names and sharing a coauthor in common would be two different persons in the real world, and also that they tend to publish in the same subjects and publication venues for some portion of their careers. The experiments also confirmed that HHC was able to produce very pure clusters with low fragmentation in the tested datasets.

---

[3] See Appendix A for more details on this function.

CHAPTER 5

SAND: Self-Training Author Name Disambiguator

In this chapter, we describe a hybrid author name disambiguation method called SAND (Self-training Author Name Disambiguator) [Ferreira et al., 2014]. SAND is an effective and highly practical method that exploits the strengths of both author grouping and author assignment approaches for addressing the author name disambiguation problem. To describe SAND, we first overview its approach (Section 5.1) and then describe each one of its three main steps: author grouping (Section 5.2), cluster selection (Section 5.3), and author assignment (Section 5.4).

5.1 OVERVIEW OF SAND

Figure 5.1 presents the three main steps of SAND, which are preceded by a preprocessing phase that aims at blocking the ambiguous authorship records. In the first step, *author grouping*, recurring patterns in the coauthorship graph are exploited in order to produce very pure clusters of authorship records. In the second step, *cluster selection*, a subset of the clusters produced in the previous step is selected as training data for the next step. Finally, in the third step, *author assignment*, a learned function is derived from the training data to disambiguate the authorship records in the clusters that were not previously selected. This last step is capable of improving the coverage of the training data by adding reliable predicted records and, in case of a doubtful prediction, the respective record returns to the test set. The final result is a highly effective and extremely practical author name disambiguation method.

The SAND steps are applied after a standard pre-processing procedure, which includes blocking, stop-word removal, and stemming. Stop-word removal and stemming are performed on the words that compose work and publication venue titles. Moreover, authors with similar ambiguous names are grouped together (i.e., blocked), creating ambiguous groups. A disambiguation procedure is then performed within each ambiguous group, so that useless comparisons involving non-ambiguous authors are avoided.

To illustrate the SAND steps, let us consider the set of authorship records shown in Figure 5.2, which are used in the discussion that follows next. This set contains ambiguous authorship records with author names similar to "A. Gupta," but that belong to three distinct researchers, namely Amit Gupta, Anupam Gupta and Alok Gupta, who, by the time their works were published, were affiliated, respectively, with the Tenet Group of the University of Califor-

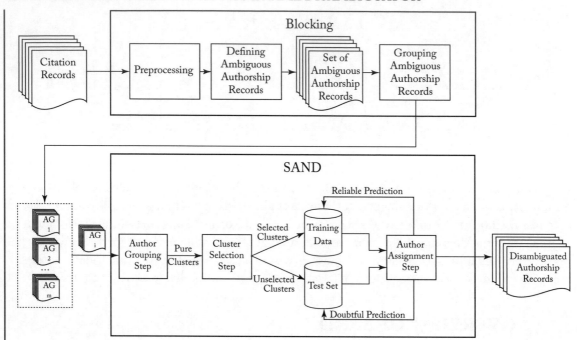

Figure 5.1: SAND overview.

nia at Berkeley, California, the Computer Science Division of the University of California at Berkeley, California, and the Siemens Corporate Research, in Princeton, New Jersey.

5.2   THE AUTHOR GROUPING STEP

The goal of this step is to automatically create pure clusters of authorship records. Some of these clusters will be chosen by the cluster selection step to compose the training data to be used in the final step. The idea is to split the set of authorship records within each ambiguous group into several clusters, so that authorship records placed in a same cluster tend to be very similar to each other and dissimilar to authorship records placed in other clusters. The key intuition behind this strategy is that some of these clusters can be associated with a unique author label and, therefore, authorship records within such clusters can serve as training examples. In order to properly produce training examples, the extracted clusters should be as pure as possible, in the sense that each cluster should contain only authorship records of a same author. Otherwise, if a cluster with a low degree of purity (i.e., a cluster with authorship records of distinct authors) were selected as training, then authorship records of different authors could be assigned to the author label associated with this cluster in the author assignment step, increasing the homonym problem.

Figure 5.2: Examples of authorship records that include the author name "A. Gupta."

To illustrate the idea of this step, consider the records shown in Figure 5.2. If we group them by coauthorship, we will obtain the clusters of authorship records showed in Figure 5.3. Notice that, for this example, it was possible to group into the same cluster (Cluster 2) three authorship records, which share the same coauthor "R. Bettati." The remaining records resulted into clusters with a single authorship record due to the lack of common coauthorships and the small size of our example. The resulting clusters are very pure, that is, each cluster has only authorship records of a same author, but there exist authorship records of the same author split into distinct clusters. For instance, Clusters 1 and 5 contain records of Alok Gupta, and records in Clusters 2 and 6 belong to Amit Gupta. Thus, this step starts the disambiguation process but does not solve it. In the next steps, SAND uses the clusters produced by its first step for automatically generating labeled examples and inferring a disambiguation function to attempt solving the name ambiguity existing among the authorship records.

A straightforward way of extracting pure clusters is to ensure that each one of them contains only a single authorship record. In this case, clusters are totally pure, but fragmentation is maximum, i.e., the authorship records of a same author are placed into different clusters. Fragmented clusters are potentially detrimental for learning the author assignment function, since authorship records of a same author would receive different labels.

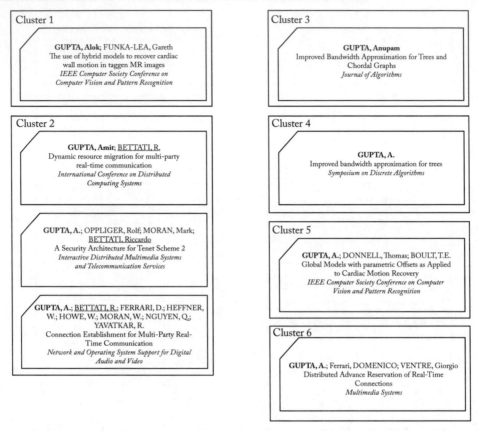

Figure 5.3: Author grouping step applied to the autorship records shown in Figure 5.2.

Accordingly, in SAND, pure clusters are extracted by exploiting highly discriminative attributes, so that authorship records associated with different authors are unlikely to be grouped together into the same cluster. Considering the realm of bibliographic citations, we have based this strategy on the same heuristic adopted in the first step of the HHC method (see Section 4.2), which assumes that very rarely two authors with similar names and coauthors in common would be two different people in the real world [Cota et al., 2010]. SAND associates two attributes to each cluster, i.e., *author* and *coauthors*, which correspond, respectively, to the author name mentioned in the first authorship record inserted into that cluster and the union of all coauthor names found in all authorship records of the same cluster.

Algorithm 5.5 describes this first step of SAND. It processes the authorship records and produces as output a list of clusters that ideally contain in each cluster only records of a same author. This algorithm is basically the same one used by HHC in its first step, but with a slightly different ProcessList function (Lines 6 and 7). Algorithm 5.6 describes this specific function,

---

Algorithm 5.5 The Author Grouping Step

Require: Ambiguous group G of authorship records;
Ensure: List $\mathcal{C}$ of clusters of authorship records;

1: Let L and S be lists of authorship records;
2: Let C_1 and C_2 be lists of clusters;
3: $S \leftarrow$ GetShortNameRecords(G);
4: $L \leftarrow$ GetLongNameRecords(G);
5: $C_1 \leftarrow \emptyset$;
6: $C_2 \leftarrow$ ProcessList(L,C_1);
7: $\mathcal{C} \leftarrow$ ProcessList(S,C_2);

Algorithm 5.6 Function ProcessList

Require: List L of authorship records;
Require: List C_i of clusters of authorship records;
Ensure: List C_o of clusters of authorship records;

1: $C_o \leftarrow C_i$;
2: **for each** r in L **do**
3:     $inserted \leftarrow$ false;
4:     $c \leftarrow$ first(C_o);
5:     **while not** $inserted$ **and** $c \neq$ **null do**
6:         **if** similar(r.authorName, c.authorName) **and** exists similar(r.coauthorNames, c.coauthorNames) **then**
7:             InsertAuthorshipRecord(r, c);
8:             $inserted \leftarrow$ true;
9:         **end if**
10:         $c \leftarrow$ next(C_o);
11:     **end while**
12:     **if** $inserted$ = **false then**
13:         $c \leftarrow$ CreateNewCluster(r);
14:         Append(C_o, c);
15:     **end if**
16: **end for**

---

which is used to process the list of authorship records. This algorithm receives a list L of authorship records and a list C_i of authorship record clusters, and then returns a new list C_o with each authorship record r from L inserted in some cluster c of C_o. It compares the author name in each authorship record r with the author name associated with each cluster c using some similarity function. If the author name of r is similar to the author name associated with c and there are coauthor names in r that are similar to some coauthor names in c, r is inserted into this cluster c (Line 7); otherwise, a new cluster is created with this authorship record r (Line 13).

Like HHC, to measure the similarity between two names, SAND uses a function derived from the Fragment Comparison algorithm [Oliveira, 2005]. To verify whether an authorship record r and a cluster c share common coauthors, SAND exploits two strategies, a weak and a strong one. The weak strategy considers that r and c share coauthors when they have at least one similar coauthor name in common. The strong strategy tries to increase the purity of the generated clusters, by building upon the first one. For this, SAND uses an external source of evidence containing the most popular last names of a given language. In this second strategy, SAND considers that r and c share coauthors if both have at least one similar coauthor whose last name is not popular or if they have at least *two* similar coauthor names (popular or not). For implementing this heuristic, SAND uses a list of popular last names created from persons' names collected from Wikipedia[1] and BDBComp (for the Brazilian Portuguese case).

Although simple, this additional constraint tends to extract even purer clusters when compared to the first strategy (for more details see the experimental evaluation reported by Ferreira et al. [2014]). Unfortunately, both strategies also tend to fragment the authorship records of an author into multiple clusters. This is expected, since some authors are likely to have many different coauthors due to multiple interests and some of these coauthors may have never published together.

5.3   THE CLUSTER SELECTION STEP

As mentioned before, if the final set of clusters to be used as training data is too fragmented, then possibly many authorship records will be associated with incorrect author labels,[2] decreasing the benefit of the training examples. One strategy to reduce fragmentation in the training data is to select only clusters that belong to different real authors.

For example, if we use the clusters shown in Figure 5.3, we may consider more representative for a given author the largest cluster with authorship records of that author, or we can use a similarity function to check if two clusters may belong to the same author. Thus, a possible strategy is to sort the clusters in descending order by the number of records and filter the dissimilar clusters to compose the training set. Figure 5.4 shows the selected clusters. For our example, the first selected cluster was Cluster 2, the largest one. Then, Clusters 1 and 3, which were considered dissimilar to Cluster 2 as well as from each other, were inserted into the training set. Thus, each selected cluster may represent an author. Looking at the work and publication venue titles from the records in Clusters 4, 5, and 6, we notice a similarity with the titles in

---

[1]http://en.wikipedia.org/wiki/Lists_of_most_common_surnames

[2]Remind that each cluster in the training data is associated with a different label. If two clusters of the same author are included in the training data, these clusters will be considered as belonging to different authors.

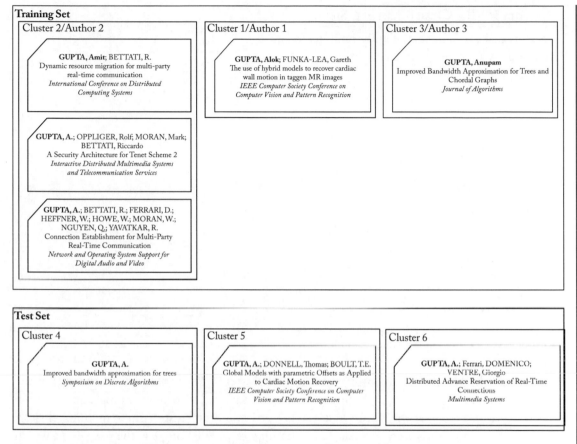

Figure 5.4: Cluster selection step applied on clusters shown in Figure 5.3.

Clusters 1, 2, and 3. For for this reason, Clusters 4, 5, and 6 were not selected and their records will compose the test set. Next, we describe Selection Step in detail.

Algorithm 5.7 selects the training examples and the test set to be processed by the next step (*author assignment*). The process of selecting the clusters whose authorship records will compose the initial training data starts by sorting the input clusters produced in the previous step (Line 3) in descending order of size (i.e., the number of authorship records within the cluster). The result is a sorted list $\mathcal{C}$ of clusters. Then, the largest cluster in $\mathcal{C}$ is inserted into the set of selected clusters, $\mathcal{S}$ (Lines 4 and 5). This selected cluster is also removed from $\mathcal{C}$. As the clusters in $\mathcal{S}$ should belong to different authors, the next cluster in $\mathcal{C}$ to be inserted into $\mathcal{S}$ should be one not similar to any of the clusters already in $\mathcal{S}$. The key intuition behind this strategy is that candidate clusters in $\mathcal{C}$ that are dissimilar to clusters in $\mathcal{S}$ are those most likely to contain authorship records associated with authors not already in $\mathcal{S}$. Thus, we insert a cluster $c_i \in \mathcal{C}$ in $\mathcal{S}$ if $\forall c_j \in \mathcal{S}$, c_i is not similar to c_j (Lines 6–11). The iteration continues with the next candidate

---

Algorithm 5.7 The Cluster Selection Step

Require: List $\mathcal{C}$ of clusters of authorship records;
Ensure: List $\mathcal{D}$ of training data;
Ensure: List $\mathcal{T}$ of test set;

  1: Let $\mathcal{S}$ be the list of selected clusters;
  2: $\mathcal{S} \leftarrow \emptyset$;
  3: $\mathcal{C} \leftarrow$ Sort($\mathcal{C}$, desc);
  4: $c_i \leftarrow$ GetFirstCluster($\mathcal{C}$);
  5: Append($\mathcal{S}, c_i$);
  6: Remove($c_i, \mathcal{C}$);
  7: **for each** c_i **in** $\mathcal{C}$ **do**
  8:    **if** $\forall c_j \in \mathcal{S}$, Dissimilar($c_i, c_j$) **then**
  9:       Append($\mathcal{S}, c_i$);
10:      Remove($c_i, \mathcal{C}$);
11:   **end if**
12: **end for**
13: $\mathcal{D} \leftarrow \mathcal{S}$;
14: $\mathcal{T} \leftarrow \mathcal{C}$;

---

cluster in $\mathcal{C}$. The process finally stops when the last cluster in $\mathcal{C}$ is evaluated. At the end of the process, authorship records in each cluster $c_j \in \mathcal{S}$ are inserted into the training data $\mathcal{D}$. Each authorship record receives the author label of the corresponding cluster. The remaining clusters whose authorship records were not selected as training data, will compose the test set $\mathcal{T}$, which will be disambiguated by the last step of SAND.

    Three strategies might be used to measure the similarity/dissimilarity among clusters [Ferreira et al., 2014]:

- *Strategy 1.* We compare two clusters c_i and c_j by using the attributes of the authorship records that compose them. Each authorship record is represented as a feature vector and a similarity function ϕ (e.g., cosine, Euclidean distance, etc.) between authorship records in clusters c_i and c_j (or between their respective centroids), is used to measure the similarity between c_i and c_j. The clusters are considered dissimilar according to the following rule:

$$Dissimilar(c_i, c_j) = \begin{cases} 1, & \text{IF } \phi(c_i, c_j) < \phi_{\min} \\ 0, & \text{OTHERWISE.} \end{cases}$$

In other words, clusters c_i and $c_j \in \mathcal{S}$ are considered not similar if the value $\phi(c_i, c_j)$ between c_i and c_j is not greater than a minimum value ($\phi_{\min}$) necessary for the clusters to be considered similar.

- *Strategy 2.* We compare two clusters c_i and c_j considering only the author names assigned to them and using some author name similarity function τ (e.g., fragment comparison) that checks whether two author names are similar (i.e., if they may refer to the same person) or not. If the cluster's author names are considered not similar according to the function τ, the respective clusters are also considered not similar:

$$Dissimilar(c_i, c_j) = \begin{cases} 1, & \text{IF NOT } \tau(c_i.authorName, c_j.authorName) \\ 0, & \text{OTHERWISE.} \end{cases}$$

- *Strategy 3.* This strategy combines both previous strategies:

$$Dissimilar(c_i, c_j) = \begin{cases} 1, & \text{IF NOT } \tau(c_i.authorName, c_j.authorName) \\ & \text{or } \phi(c_i, c_j) < \phi_{\min} \\ 0, & \text{OTHERWISE.} \end{cases}$$

As options for the function ϕ, one can exploit the cosine similarity function and the euclidean distance that are metrics frequently used to measure the similarity or dissimilarity between vectors. For cluster similarity, four options are possible [Ferreira et al., 2014]: similarity between the respective cluster centroids as well as single, complete and average linkage (described next). This encompasses eight possible combinations of similarity function and cluster similarity strategies. Next, we describe the similarity metrics in more detail, in which each authorship record r is represented as a feature vector $\vec{r}$.

Cosine Similarity.   The cosine similarity function [Salton et al., 1975] is given by the following formula:

$$cosine\left(\vec{r}_i, \vec{r}_j\right) = \frac{\sum_k r_{ik} \cdot r_{jk}}{|\vec{r}_i| \cdot |\vec{r}_j|},$$

where

- $\vec{r}_i$ and $\vec{r}_j$ correspond to the feature vectors of authorship records r_i and r_j, respectively;

- $|\vec{r}|$ corresponds to the norm of the vector $\vec{r}$; and

- r_{ik} and r_{jk} correspond to the value of k-th feature in the vectors $\vec{r}_i$ and $\vec{r}_j$, respectively.

Euclidian Distance.   The Euclidian distance [Jain et al., 1999] between two vectors is calculated by the following formula:

$$euclidean\_distance\left(\vec{r}_i, \vec{r}_j\right) = \sqrt{\sum_{k=1}^{n} \left(r_{ik} - r_{jk}\right)^2}.$$

We change the euclidean distance to use it as a similarity metric by applying the following formula:

$$euclidean\left(\vec{r}_i, \vec{r}_j\right) = 1 - \frac{euclidean\_distance\left(\vec{r}_i, \vec{r}_j\right)}{euclian\_distance_{max}},$$

where $euclidean\_distance_{max}$ corresponds to the largest distance between all vectors.

Cluster Similarity Strategies.   Ferreira et al. [2014] evaluated four similarity strategies specially designed for clustering tasks [Jain et al., 1999], which are based on (1) the centroids of the clusters, (2) single-link, (3) complete-link, and (4) average-link. The similarities between two clusters c_i and c_j are calculated by using the following formulas:

- Centroid:

$$centroid(c_i, c_j) = \phi\left(\vec{r}_i, \vec{r}_j\right),$$

  where $\vec{r}_i$ and $\vec{r}_j$ are the centroids from c_i and c_j, respectively, and $\vec{r}_i = \frac{1}{|c_i|}\sum_{r \in c_i}(\vec{r})$.

- Single-link:

$$single(c_i, c_j) = \phi\left(\vec{r}_i, \vec{r}_j\right),$$

  where $\vec{r}_i$ and $\vec{r}_j$ are the vectors from c_i and c_j, respectively, that have the highest similarity.

- Complete-link:

$$complete(c_i, c_j) = \phi\left(\vec{r}_i, \vec{r}_j\right),$$

  where $\vec{r}_i$ and $\vec{r}_j$ are the vectors from c_i and c_j, respectively, that have the lowest similarity.

- Average-link:

$$average(c_i, c_j) = \frac{\sum_{\vec{r}_i \in c_i} \sum_{\vec{r}_j \in c_j} \phi\left(\vec{r}_i, \vec{r}_j\right)}{|c_i| * |c_j|},$$

  where $\phi(\vec{r}_i, \vec{r}_j)$ can be calculated by using any similarity metric between two vectors.

5.4   THE AUTHOR ASSIGNMENT STEP

In the third and final step of SAND, the set of examples $\mathcal{D}$ is used to produce a disambiguation function from $\{f_1, f_2, \ldots, f_m\}$ to $\{a_1, a_2, \ldots, a_n\}$ that is used to predict the correct author of the authorship records in the test set $\mathcal{T}$. In this case, the test set $\mathcal{T}$ is composed of all authorship records not belonging to clusters selected in the previous step. The idea is that, with the training set selected in the previous step, we would be able to learn an assignment function that will correctly predict the authors of these remaining authorship records. For those authors in the collection without a representative cluster in the training data $\mathcal{D}$, SAND will (hopefully) detect them as new authors and include them in the training for later use, i.e., the method is also self-trained. Then, the idea of this step is to assign each authorship record from the test set to an

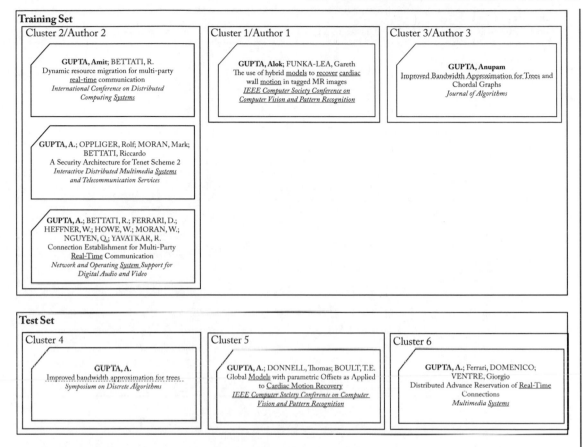

Figure 5.5: Result of the author assignment step.

author represented by a cluster in the training set or, otherwise, to identify the authorship record as belonging to a new author.

Thus, looking at Figure 5.5, we notice that the authorship record in Cluster 4 has some title terms similar to the title terms of the record in Cluster 3, which means that a disambiguation function using these terms as features should be able to assign the record from Cluster 4 to Cluster 3, i.e., the author in Cluster 3 is most likely the same author of the record in Cluster 4. Considering the record in Cluster 5, its work title and publication venue share terms with those of Cluster 1 (Author 1) and the record in Cluster 6 shares terms from its work and publication venue titles with those of the records in Cluster 2 (Author 2). Thus, a disambiguation function should be able to assign the record from Cluster 4 to Cluster 3 (Author 3), the record from Cluster 5 to Cluster 1 (Author 1) and the record from Cluster 6 to Cluster 2 (Author 2), thus resulting in the new training set shown in Figure 5.6, if all predictions are reliable. The process executed in this step stops when the test set finally gets empty.

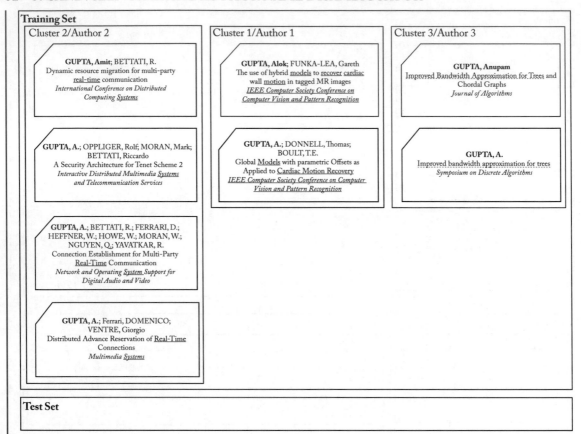

Figure 5.6: Final result of the author assignment step.

Next, we describe in more detail some specific issues regarding the author assignment step, which produces disambiguation functions from the set of examples $\mathcal{D}$ based on a lazy associative classifier [Veloso et al., 2006b].

5.4.1 ASSOCIATIVE NAME DISAMBIGUATION

The proposed technique for deriving a disambiguation function exploits the fact that, frequently, there are strong associations between features $\{f_1, f_2, \ldots, f_m\}$ and specific authors $\{a_1, a_2, \ldots, a_n\}$. The proposed technique uncovers such associations from $\mathcal{D}$, and then produces a disambiguation function $\{f_1, f_2, \ldots, f_m\} \rightarrow \{a_1, a_2, \ldots, a_n\}$ using such associations [Veloso et al., 2006b]. Typically, these associations are expressed using rules of the form $\mathcal{X} \rightarrow a_1$, $\mathcal{X} \rightarrow a_2, \ldots, \mathcal{X} \rightarrow a_n$, where $\mathcal{X} \subseteq \{f_1, f_2, \ldots, f_m\}$. In the following discussion, we denote as $\mathcal{R}$ an arbitrary rule set. Similarly, we denote as $\mathcal{R}_{a_i}$ a subset of $\mathcal{R}$ that is composed of rules of the form $\mathcal{X} \rightarrow a_i$ (i.e., rules predicting author a_i). A rule $\mathcal{X} \rightarrow a_i$ is said to match a authorship record x if $\mathcal{X} \subseteq x$ (i.e., x contains all features in $\mathcal{X}$) and this rule is included in $\mathcal{R}^x_{a_i}$. That is, $\mathcal{R}^x_{a_i}$ is composed of rules predicting author a_i and matching authorship record x. Obviously, $\mathcal{R}^x_{a_i} \subseteq \mathcal{R}_{a_i} \subseteq \mathcal{R}$.

Example: Consider the Cluster 1 shown in Figure 5.4 for representing the author a_1 (Author 1), whose authorship record has some features such as "coauthor=g.funka-lea," "work=hybrid," "work=model," "work=cardiac," "venue=vision," "venue=pattern," and so on. Thus, to predict a_1, we may consider, for instance, the following rules:

"coauthor=g.funka-lea" $\rightarrow a_1$
"work=cardiac" $\rightarrow a_1$
"venue=vision" $\rightarrow a_1$
"coauthor=g.funka-lea", "work=cardiac" $\rightarrow a_1$
"coauthor=g.funka-lea", "work=cardiac", "venue=vision" $\rightarrow a_1$

Notice, for instance, that the rules "work=cardiac" $\rightarrow a_1$ and "venue=vision" $\rightarrow a_1$ match the authorship record in the Cluster 5 showed in Figure 5.4 and, thus, belong to the rule set $\mathcal{R}^x_{a_1}$ of that record. These rules indicate that if the work title contains the term "cardiac" or the publication venue title contains the term "vision," there exists a confidence of a_1 being the author associated with the authorship record in Cluster 5. Thus, a disambiguation function will use the rules in $\mathcal{R}^x_{a_1}$ to infer the probability of a_1 being the author associated with the authorship record x.

5.4.2 DEMAND-DRIVEN RULE EXTRACTION

Rule extraction is a major issue for associative name disambiguation, since the number of extracted rules may increase exponentially with the number of features in the training data. This method, however, extracts rules from the training data on a demand-driven fashion [Veloso et al., 2006a], at disambiguation time. It projects the search space for rules according to information in the authorship records in $\mathcal{T}$, thus providing an efficient rule extraction. In other words, the proposed method projects/filters the training data according to the features in an authorship record $x \in \mathcal{T}$, and extracts rules from this projected training data, which is denoted as $\mathcal{D}^x$. This ensures that only rules that carry information about authorship the record x are extracted from the training data, drastically limiting the number of possible rules. Lines 1–5 of Algorithm 5.8 describe this projection.

5.4.3 PREDICTING THE AUTHOR OF EACH AUTHORSHIP RECORD

Naturally, there is a total ordering among the rules, in the sense that some rules show stronger associations than others. A widely used statistic, called confidence [Agrawal et al., 1993] (denoted by $\theta(\mathcal{X} \rightarrow a_i)$), measures the strength of the association between $\mathcal{X}$ and a_i. More specifically, the confidence of the rule $\mathcal{X} \rightarrow a_i$ is given by the conditional probability of a_i being the author of the authorship record x, given that $\mathcal{X} \subseteq x$.

Algorithm 5.8 Associative Name Disambiguation

Require: Examples in $\mathcal{D}$ and authorship record $x \in \mathcal{T}$
Ensure: The predicted author of the authorship record x

1: Let $\mathcal{L}(f_i)$ be the set of examples in $\mathcal{D}$ in which feature f_i has occurred
2: $\mathcal{D}^x \Leftarrow \emptyset$
3: **for each** feature $f_i \in x$ **do**
4:    $\mathcal{D}^x \Leftarrow \mathcal{D}^x \cup \mathcal{L}(f_i)$
5: **end for**
6: **for each** author a_i **do**
7:    $\mathcal{R}^x_{a_i} \Leftarrow$ rules $\mathcal{X} \rightarrow a_i$ extracted from $\mathcal{D}^x$
8:    Estimate $\hat{p}(a_i|x)$, according to Equation (5.2)
9: **end for**
10: Predict author a_i such that $\hat{p}(a_i|c) > \hat{p}(a_j|c) \forall j \neq i$

Using a single rule to predict the correct author may be prone to error. Instead, the probability (or likelihood) of a_i being the author of the authorship record x is estimated by combining rules in $\mathcal{R}^x_{a_i}$. More specifically, $\mathcal{R}^x_{a_i}$ is interpreted as a poll, in which each rule $\mathcal{X} \rightarrow a_i \in \mathcal{R}^x_{a_i}$ is a vote given by features in $\mathcal{X}$ for author a_i. The weight of a vote $\mathcal{X} \rightarrow a_i$ depends on the strength of the association between $\mathcal{X}$ and a_i, which is given by $\theta(\mathcal{X} \rightarrow a_i)$. The process of estimating the probability of a_i being the author of authorship record x starts by summing weighted votes for a_i and then averaging the obtained value by the total number of votes for a_i, as expressed by the score function $s(a_i, x)$ shown in Equation (5.1) (where $r_j \subseteq \mathcal{R}^x_{a_i}$ and $|\mathcal{R}^x_{a_i}|$ is the number of rules in $\mathcal{R}^x_{a_i}$). Thus, $s(a_i, x)$ gives the average confidence of the rules in $\mathcal{R}^x_{a_i}$ (obviously, the higher the confidence, the stronger the evidence of the authorship).

$$s(a_i, x) = \frac{\sum_{j=1}^{|\mathcal{R}^x_{a_i}|} \theta(r_j)}{|\mathcal{R}^x_{a_i}|}. \tag{5.1}$$

The estimated probability of a_i being the author represented in an authorship record x, denoted as $\hat{p}(a_i|x)$, is simply obtained by normalizing $s(a_i, x)$, as shown in Equation (5.2). A higher value of $\hat{p}(a_i|x)$ indicates a higher likelihood of a_i being the author of x. The author associated with the highest likelihood is finally predicted as the author of the authorship record x. Lines 6–10 of Algorithm 5.8 describe the prediction of the author of each authorship record.

$$\hat{p}(a_i|x) = \frac{s(a_i, x)}{\sum_{j=1}^{n} s(a_j, x)}. \tag{5.2}$$

5.4.4   EXPLOITING RELIABLE PREDICTIONS

Additional examples may be obtained from the predictions performed using the disambiguation function. In this case, reliable predictions are regarded as correct ones and, thus, they can be safely included in the training examples. Next, we define the *reliability* of a prediction.

Given an arbitrary authorship record $x \in \mathcal{T}$, and the two most likely authors for x, a_i, and a_j, we denote as $\Delta(x)$ the reliability of predicting a_i, as shown in Equation (5.3).

$$\Delta(x) = \frac{\hat{p}(a_i|x)}{\hat{p}(a_j|x)}. \tag{5.3}$$

The idea is to only predict a_i if $\Delta(x) \geq \Delta_{\min}$, where $\Delta_{\min}$ is a threshold that indicates the minimum reliability necessary to regard the corresponding prediction as correct, and, therefore, to include it into the training data $\mathcal{D}$. An appropriate value for $\Delta_{\min}$ can be obtained by performing a cross-validation [Geisser, 1993], which is a way to predict the fit of a disambiguation function to a hypothetical validation set.

5.4.5   TEMPORARY ABSTENTION

Naturally, some predictions are not enough reliable for certain values of $\Delta_{\min}$. An alternative is to abstain from such doubtful predictions. As new examples are included into $\mathcal{D}$ (i.e., the reliable predictions), new evidence may be exploited, hopefully increasing the reliability of the predictions that were previously abstained. To optimize the usage of reliable predictions, we place authorship records in a queue, so that authorship records associated with reliable predictions are considered first. The process works as follows. Initially, authorship records in the test set are randomly placed in the queue. If the author of the authorship record that is located in the beginning of the queue can be reliably predicted, then the prediction is performed, the authorship record is removed from the queue and included into $\mathcal{D}$ as a new example. Otherwise, if the prediction is not reliable, the corresponding authorship record is simply placed in the end of the queue and will be only processed after all other authorship records. The process continues performing more reliable predictions first, until no more reliable predictions are possible. The remaining authorship records in $\mathcal{T}$ (for which only doubtful predictions are possible) are then processed normally, but the corresponding predictions are not included into $\mathcal{D}$. The process stops after all authorship records in $\mathcal{T}$ have been processed.

5.4.6   DETECTING NEW AUTHORS

We propose to use the lack of rules supporting any already seen author (i.e., authors that are present in some authorship record in $\mathcal{D}$) as evidence indicating the appearance of an unseen author. The number of rules that is necessary to consider an author as an already seen one is controlled by a parameter, $\gamma_{\min}$. Specifically, for an authorship record $x \in \mathcal{T}$, if the number of rules extracted from $\mathcal{D}^x$ (which is denoted as $\gamma(x)$) is smaller than $\gamma_{\min}$ (i.e., $\gamma(x) < \gamma_{\min}$), then the author of x is considered as a new/unseen author and a new label a_k is created to identify such author. Further, this prediction is considered as a new example and included into $\mathcal{D}$. An appropriate value for $\gamma_{\min}$ can be obtained by performing cross-validation in $\mathcal{D}$.

5.4.7   PREDICTING THE AUTHOR OF EACH CLUSTER

Alternatively, instead of predicting the author of each authorship record, we could explore some of the work already done in the author grouping step in order to directly predict the author of the cluster, i.e., all authorship records in a cluster $c \in \mathcal{T}$ would be assigned to the same author label avoiding to assign some of the authorship records within the cluster to other authors. This can only be done in an effective way if most of the clusters are pure, because mixed authorship records in a cluster could not be fixed later.

To predict the author of a cluster c, we first predict the authors of each authorship record $r \in c$. After that, we use the parameter $\Delta_{\min}$ and the number of authorship records of the two most oftenly predicted authors, a_i and a_j, in c. Let these numbers be n_i and n_j, respectively. If $\frac{n_i}{n_j} > \Delta_{\min}$, we consider the cluster c as belonging to author a_i and each authorship record $r \in c$ is assigned to author a_i. Otherwise, we assign the authorship records in c to a new author. After the prediction of the cluster c, its authorship records are inserted into the training data $\mathcal{D}$.

5.5   FINAL COMMENTS

SAND was designed for exploiting the strengths of both unsupervised author grouping and supervised author assignment approaches. With respect to its complexity, SAND depends on its rule generation process for identifying the author of each authorship record. According to Veloso et al. [2012], the extraction of rules increases polynomially with the number of features n in the training data. Since an authorship record x has at most k features ($k \ll n$), any useful rule for predicting the author of x has at most k features in its antecedent. Thus, the number of rules for predicting the author of x is $a \times (k + \binom{k}{2} + \cdots + \binom{k}{k}) = O(a \times n^k)$, where a is the total number of authors.

In our experimental evaluation [Ferreira et al., 2014], using the Cota-DBLP and Cota-BDBComp datasets, as well as synthetic data generated by SyGAR (see Appendix B), we compared SAND with two author assignment methods based, respectively, on the naïve Bayes probability model and on SVM [Han et al., 2004]. We also compared SAND with three author grouping methods, HHC (described in Chapter 4) and those based on the K-way spectral clustering technique [Han et al., 2005b] and on an online SVM algorithm applied together with the DBScan clustering technique [Huang et al., 2006]. The experimental results demonstrated the superiority of SAND over all baselines but HHC, with which SAND statistically tied in the Cota-BDBComp dataset, considering both, the K and pF1 metrics.

When simulating the addition of new authors using data generated by SyGAR, SAND and HHC remained basically tied. However, when simulating changes in the authors' profiles at each new load on the repository, SAND performed much better than all the other methods, showing that it is the most resilient among all tested methods, independently of the level of profile change.

CHAPTER 6

Incremental Author Name Disambiguation

With Ana Paula de Carvalho and Alan Filipe Santana

In this chapter, we address two incremental author name disambiguation methods, namely INDi (Incremental Unsupervised Name Disambiguator) [de Carvalho et al., 2011] and INC (Incremental Nearest Cluster) [Santana et al., 2017]. Unlike more traditional methods such those described in Chapters 4 and 5, incremental author name disambiguation methods provide strategies that guarantee the correct authorship assignment of new citation records as they are added to a bibliographic repository, thus avoiding the disambiguation of its entire repository from time to time. In what follows, we first describe INDi (Section 6.1) and then INC (Section 6.2), finishing the chapter with a brief discussion on the complexity of both methods (Section 6.3).

6.1 INDI – INCREMENTAL UNSUPERVISED NAME DISAMBIGUATOR

INDi aims at determining the authors of new citation records added to a bibliographic repository, thus avoiding the disambiguation of the entire repository. For doing so, it uses some heuristics to disambiguate the author names (i.e., the authorship records) of new citation records. These heuristics are meant to disambiguate these new records by prioritizing the assignment of them to correct authors. Thus, in case of any doubts, INDi considers these new records as belonging to a new author (i.e., an author that does not have yet any citation record in the bibliographic repository), instead of assigning a doubtful record to an existing author with a probability of error. In this sense, INDi has a bias toward producing groups (clusters) of citations that are very pure, which means that most of the citation records assigned by INDi to a given existing author are likely to be correct. The side effect of this strategy is that authors who are not so prolific and, therefore, have few entries in the repository, may have their publications split into groups associated with new authors. This is done for a major reason: mixing the citation records of different authors is a much harder problem to fix than putting together split groups by a manual correction procedure,[1] which it is assumed that will eventually occur given that current

---

[1]Although post-clustering surveillance techniques [Xu and Wunsch, 2005], e.g., resampling of authorship records from clusters, could be applied to ameliorate the problem, it is still a difficult task.

state-of-the-art methods still do produce errors. In fact, it is much easier for the administrator of a bibliographic repository to check whether the authors indicated as new by a disambiguation method are in fact of this type, than sorting through all the groups already in the repository to find eventual errors. Therefore, INDi is an incremental method that disambiguates only new entries, being capable of benefiting from eventual manual corrections.

In more details, INDi attempts to disambiguate new citation records by looking for an author whose authorship records already existing in the bibliographic repository have a similar author name, at least one coauthor in common and similar work or publication venue titles. Figure 6.1 shows the example of a new citation with eight author names to disambiguate, thus generating eight authorship records. To simplify the discussion, let us consider the authorship record whose author name is "Gupta, A.," which refers to Amit Gupta as listed on DBLP.[2] This record has three candidate authors in the bibliographic repository, corresponding to Clusters 1, 2, and 3. Notice that this new record shares its coauthor name and work title terms with the authorship records from Cluster 2. Based on such evidence, INDi will add this new authorship record to Cluster 2.

For those cases in which the new citation record does not include any coauthor (i.e., citations records with a single author) or when all existing authorship records from the group of an author with a similar name do not have coauthors, we avoid the coauthor check, but raise similarity thresholds for publication venue and work title. Figures 6.2 and 6.3 illustrate these cases. In Figure 6.2, the authorship record refers to a distinct researcher called Anupam Gupta, as listed on DBLP,[3] and corresponds to a new citation that does not have coauthors, but whose work title is very similar to the one from the authorship record belonging to Cluster 3. Thus, INDi adds the authorship record from this new citation to Cluster 3. In Figure 6.3, the authorship records from Cluster 3 do not have coauthors, but one of them refers to the same publication venue included in the authorship record of the new citation. Notice that, when all the previous tests fail, the authorship record is considered as belonging to a new author. The alternative to these last steps, i.e., to consider as evidence only the similarity of the work and publication venue titles when there is no coauthors in common, would most probably incur in many false positives, thus decreasing the purity of the groups, a situation that we certainly want to avoid.

The main steps of INDi are described by Algorithm 6.9 [de Carvalho et al., 2011]. This algorithm receives as input a new citation record c and an existing collection $\mathcal{C}$ of citation records, presumably disambiguated, in which c will be inserted, as well as two similarity thresholds α_{Venue} and α_{Title} that are used when comparing publication venue titles and work titles, respectively, and a δ value that is used to increase the similarity thresholds. The result is a list of authorship records with their corresponding authors properly identified.

---

[2]https://dblp.org/pers/hd/g/Gupta:Amit (as of July 2019).
[3]https://dblp.org/pers/hd/g/Gupta:Anupam (as of July 2019).

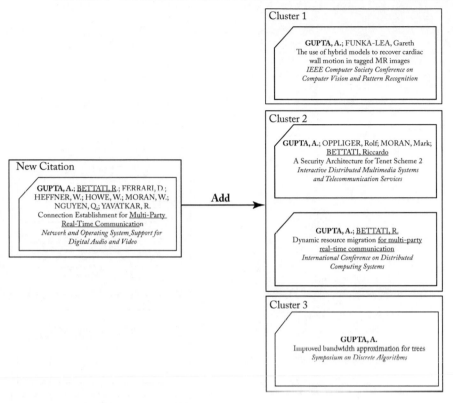

Figure 6.1: Illustrative INDi example: Step 1.

First, INDi preprocesses the citation record c by removing punctuations and stop-words from the work and publication venue titles, and stems the work title[4] (Line 1). For each authorship record r extracted from the citation record c, INDi gets from the collection C all clusters of authorship records with author names similar to the one of the authorship record r and preprocesses them (Lines 3 and 4). Then, it searches for the author of the authorship record r following three steps (Lines 5 to 23). In Step 1 (Lines 5 and 6), it searches for a cluster s that has an author name similar to the one in the authorship record r. This candidate cluster must have at least one coauthor in common with r and either a work or publication venue title similar to r. If a cluster with these characteristics is found, the authorship record r is assigned to it, which means that its author has been properly identified. We notice that this procedure follows two real-world-based heuristics similar to those adopted by the HHC method [Cota et al., 2010]: (1) very rarely two authors with similar names that share a coauthor in common would be two different people in the real world and (2) authors tend to publish on the same subjects and venues for some portion of their careers.

[4]The original INDi implementation uses the Porter's stemming algorithm [Porter, 1980].

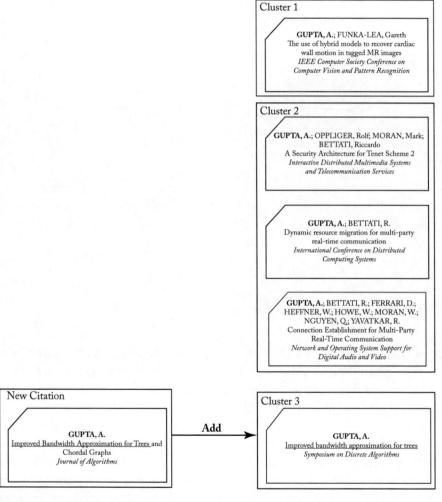

Figure 6.2: Illustrative INDi example: Step 2.

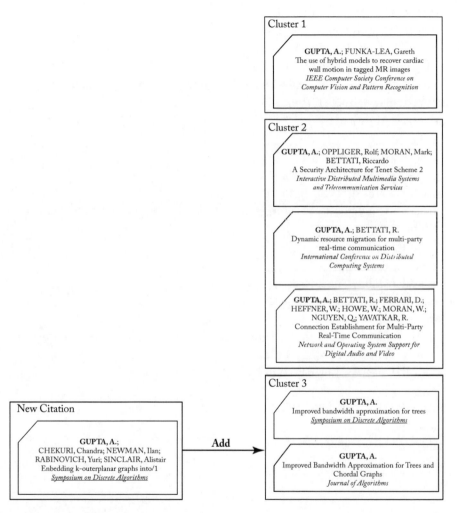

Figure 6.3: Illustrative INDi example: Step 3.

Algorithm 6.9 INDi

Require: Citation record c; Cleaned collection $\mathcal{C}$ of authorship records; Similarity thresholds α_{Venue} and α_{Title}; Incremental value δ;

Ensure: List L of pairs that contain the authorship record and the author identification;

1: $c' \leftarrow$ PreprocessCitationRecord(c);
2: **for each** authorship record $r \in c'$ **do**
3:    $S \leftarrow$ GetClustersOfSimilarAuthors(r, $\mathcal{C}$);
4:    $S' \leftarrow$ PreprocessClusters(S);
5:    **if** there is cluster $s \in S'$ **and** similarCoauthors(s, r) **and** (similarTitle(s, r, α_{Title}) **or** similarVenue(s, r, α_{Venue})) **then**
6:       add(L,r,s.AuthorId);
7:    **else**
8:       $\alpha'_{Venue} \leftarrow \alpha_{Venue} + \delta$;
9:       $\alpha'_{Title} \leftarrow \alpha_{Title} + \delta$;
10:      **if** r.coauthorList is empty **then**
11:         **if** there is cluster $s \in S'$ **and** (similarTitle(s, r, α'_{Title}) **or** similarVenue(s, r, α'_{Venue})) **then**
12:           add(L,r,s.AuthorId);
13:         **else**
14:           add(L,r,newAuthorId());
15:         **end if**
16:      **else**
17:         **if** there is $s \in S'$ **and** s.coauthorList is empty **and** (similarTitle(s, r, α'_{Title}) **or** similarVenue(s, r, α'_{Venue})) **then**
18:           add(L,r,s.AuthorId);
19:         **else**
20:           add(L,r,newAuthorId());
21:         **end if**
22:      **end if**
23:    **end if**
24: **end for**

If the above test fails, in Step 2 (Lines 10–15) INDi checks the coauthor list of the authorship record. If this list is empty (i.e., the work has a sole author), it searches for a cluster with authorship records similar to r, using for this its work or publication venue title. If this cluster is found, the authorship record r is assigned to its author, otherwise a new cluster is created to represent this author. However, if the coauthor list of the authorship record r is not empty, Step 3 (Lines 17–21) is then executed and tests whether there is a cluster s with an empty coauthor list that is similar to r using work or publication venue titles. If this test is true, the authorship record r is assigned to cluster s (Line 18), otherwise it is assigned to a new cluster (Line 20).

Notice that in Steps 2 (Lines 10–15) and 3 (Lines 17–21) the thresholds used to verify the similarity between work or publication venue titles are increased by a δ value (Lines 8 and 9). The intuition behind this threshold increase is to find work or publication venue titles more similar to those in the authorship record r, since the authorship record r or the cluster s does not include any coauthors, which would provide a stronger evidence. If all the tests in Steps 1–3 fail, we include r as belonging to a new author.

For comparing author and coauthor names, INDi uses the Fragment Comparison function [Oliveira, 2005] (see Appendix A), whereas for comparing work and publication venue titles it uses the cosine similarity function [Salton et al., 1975]. INDi also uses each word in the work or publication venue titles as a term, and calculates the cosine similarity between a cluster[5] and an authorship record derived from the new citation record by using feature vectors, in which each feature corresponds to the TF-IDF (i.e., term frequency and inverse document frequency) value of its corresponding term.[6] If the similarity is greater than a given threshold, INDi assigns the record to the respective cluster.

As INDi may produce several clusters whose authorship records eventually belong to a same author, Esperidião et al. [2014] have proposed a strategy to merge compatible clusters based on a newly inserted citation record. This strategy aims to reduce fragmentation during the insertion of this new citation record by merging clusters compatible with some of its authorship records. It is based on the assumption that if a newly inserted authorship record has a high probability of belonging to some existing clusters, then there is also a high likelihood that these clusters belong to a same author. Thus, these clusters should be merged to decrease fragmentation in the repository.

Algorithm 6.10 describes this merging strategy, which will be further referred to as MINDi. It receives as input a set of clusters A of authorship records and a newly inserted citation record c. After a preprocessing step (Line 1), i.e., removal of stop-words and stemming of the work and publication venue titles, the algorithm generates, for each authorship record r from a citation record c, a list of candidate clusters A' (Line 3), i.e., clusters whose representative author name is similar to r's author name. Next, the algorithm selects a set of clusters S from A' that likely contains authorship records from the same author of r (Line 4) using all attributes. If S is empty, the algorithm considers r as belonging to a new author (Lines 5–7), otherwise it merges all clusters from S into a (Lines 8–14). Finally, it inserts the authorship record r in a (Line 16).

A cluster a is compatible to an authorship record r if a includes authorship records with common coauthors and similar work or publication venue titles. Algorithm 6.11 also uses α_{Title} and α_{Venue} to check the similarity of titles. If r or a has no coauthors, the function only checks the

---

[5]This cluster is represented by a summary vector of all its authorship records.
[6]Term frequencies are considered within a cluster, i.e., a term may be counted multiple times if it appears in several work or publication venue titles of different citation records in the same cluster.

Algorithm 6.10 MINDi

Require: Set of clusters A of authorship records; Citation record c;
Ensure: Set of clusters A of authorship records;
  1: $c' \leftarrow$ preprocessCitationRecord(c);
  2: **for each** authorship record $r \in c'$ **do**
  3:      $A' \leftarrow$ getCandidateClusters(A, r);
  4:      $S \leftarrow$ selectClusters(A', r);
  5:      **if** $S = \emptyset$ **then**
  6:          $a \leftarrow$ newCluster();
  7:          $A \leftarrow A \cup \{a\}$;
  8:      **else**
  9:          $A \leftarrow A - S$;
 10:          $a \leftarrow \emptyset$;
 11:          **for each** cluster $s \in S$ **do**
 12:              $a \leftarrow a \cup s$;
 13:          **end for**
 14:          $A \leftarrow A \cup \{a\}$;
 15:      **end if**
 16:      add(a, r);
 17: **end for**

Algorithm 6.11 Comparison Function

Require: Cluster a of authorship records; Authorship record r; Similarity thresholds α_{Venue} and α_{Title}; An incremental value δ;
  1: **if** similarAuthorName(a, r) **then**
  2:      **if** similarCoauthors(a, r) **and** (similarTitle(a, r, α_{Title}) **or** similarVenue(a, r, α_{Venue})) **then**
  3:          **return** TRUE;
  4:      **else**
  5:          **if** r.coauthorList is empty **or** a.coauthorList is empty **then**
  6:              $auxThresVenue \leftarrow \alpha_{Venue} + \delta$;
  7:              $auxThresTitle \leftarrow \alpha_{Title} + \delta$;
  8:              **if** (similarTitle($a, r, auxThresTitle$) **or** similarVenue($a, r, auxThresVenue$)) **then**
  9:                  **return** TRUE;
 10:              **else**
 11:                  **return** FALSE;
 12:              **end if**
 13:          **else**
 14:              **return** FALSE;
 15:          **end if**
 16:      **end if**
 17: **else**
 18:      **return** FALSE;
 19: **end if**

---

similarity between work titles or publication venue titles as previously proposed by de Carvalho et al. [2011]. In this case, it increases the similarity thresholds, α_{Title} and α_{Venue}, by a factor δ (Lines 5–9) to strength the similarity requirements for inserting r into a.

The goal of this merging strategy is to identify fragmented clusters using only the authorship records from the new inserted record. If these clusters are merged, we decrease fragmentation and avoid disambiguating the entire repository. As cluster purity is a concern, first the *selectClusters* function selects a cluster a similar to an authorship record r using the given thresholds to compare work and publication venue titles. To select other clusters, we increase these thresholds by a δ factor. The more authorship records from the clusters we use to compare with the new inserted record, the higher the chance of merging clusters of different authors, thus decreasing the repository purity. Esperidião et al. [2014] evaluated five strategies to select representative authorship records from each cluster to use in this comparison. Among them, a filter applied to the authorship records in each cluster, selecting those ones closer to the centroid of the clusters, produced good results.

6.2   INC – INCREMENTAL NEAREST CLUSTER

In this section, we describe INC (Incremental Nearest Cluster) [Santana et al., 2017], an author name disambiguation method that extends a previously proposed solution [Santana et al., 2015] to address the incremental scenario. INC represents citation records as a set of terms that occur in two specific lists: one of author names and the other one of publication and venue titles. In the list of author names, each name is treated as a term. Terms in the list of publication and venue titles are obtained after the removal of stopwords and the stemming of the remaining words. For the equations defined next, we consider the notation presented in Table 6.1.

6.2.1   THE INC MODEL

INC is based on a model that exploits a set of domain specific heuristics for the author name ambiguity problem. Specifically, these heuristics are used to:

- Define a similarity function between an author (cluster) and a citation. This similarity function considers specific characteristics of the author name ambiguity problem such as:

    - differences in importance of each citation attribute (usually, coauthor names are more discriminative than work titles, which are then more discriminative than venue titles);

    - the high dimensionality of the data; and

    - the scarcity of discriminative information in each cluster. Usually most authors have only few publications, while few authors have many.

    As shown by Santana et al. [2015], this function provides better results than traditional similarity functions (e.g., cosine similarity) used in problems such as deduplication [Gruenheid et al., 2014] that exploit highly dimensional textual features.

- Decide whether to create a new cluster to represent a new author not currently in the repository.

- Correct possible misclassifications. INC checks a confidence metric that uses the similarity values obtained during the disambiguation process to decide whether an authorship record

Table 6.1: Adopted notation

Notation	Description
$c_i = c_i^a \cup c_i^c \cup c_i^t \cup c_i^v$	An authorship record represented as sets of terms for the ambiguous author name (ℓ_i), coauthors (ε_i), and publication and venue titles (ℓ_i and ℓ_i, respectively).
$c_i^x = \{t_l, t_m, \ldots\}$	An authorship record attribute represented as a set of terms.
$a_i = \{c_l, c_m, \ldots\}$	An author i represented as a group of authorship records.
$a_i^x = \{c_l^x, c_m^x, \ldots\}$	A set of terms obtained from an attribute $x \in \{a, c, t, v\}$ of the authorship records in a_i.
$\mathcal{A} = \{a_1, a_2, \ldots a_n\}$	The set of authors defined in the training data.
$\mathcal{D} = \cup_{i=1}^n a_i$	The set of authorship records in the training data.
$n_i = \lvert\{a_j : a_j, \in A \wedge \exists c_l \in a_j, t_i \in c_l\}\rvert$	The number of authors that used the term t_i in some authorship record.
w_a, w_c, w_t, w_v	Weights assigned to the author's name, coauthors' names, and publication and venue titles, respectively.

must be reclassified or not. This is important to deal with the high level of uncertainty in the author name disambiguation task (usually higher than in other related problems).

- Identify whether two or more clusters represent the same author. This is a very important aspect of the of the problem at hand, since fragmentation of an author's cluster is a very common issue. However, the fusion of similar clusters needs to be done very carefully since, once two clusters are fused, it is extremely difficult to correct this mistake, which considerably affects cluster purity.

Applying INC involves three phases: (i) selection of candidate clusters; (ii) estimation of the similarity between each authorship record and a candidate cluster; and (iii) update of the training set. The last phase involves the following steps: (a) identification of new authors; (b) identification of fragmented clusters; and (c) update of doubtful citation records. Each phase exploits several domain-specific heuristics, aiming at automatically producing a training set to be used to identify the author associated with each authorship record. The main steps of each phase are described by Algorithm 6.12 and detailed next.

Algorithm 6.12 Incremental Name Disambiguation

Require: Training set $\mathcal{A}$, authorship record c_k, set of doubtful authorship records $\mathcal{E}$
Ensure: Associate an author a_l with an authorship record c_k

1: $\mathcal{G} \leftarrow \emptyset$ {Set of clusters related to c_k}
2: **for all** $a_j \in A$ **do**
3:      **if** $matchByFragmentComparison(c_k^a, a_j^a)$ **then**
4:          Calculate $sim(c_k, a_j)$ according to Equation (6.1)
5:          **if** $sim(c_k, a_j) > 0$ **then**
6:              $\mathcal{G} \leftarrow \mathcal{G} \cup \{a_j\}$
7:          **end if**
8:      **end if**
9: **end for**
10: Let a_l be the author with the highest similarity
11: **if** $sim(c_k, a_l) \leq \gamma$ **then**
12:      $a_z \leftarrow \{c_k\}$
13:      $\mathcal{A} \leftarrow \mathcal{A} \cup \{a_z\}$
14:      $\mathcal{E} \leftarrow \mathcal{E} \cup \{c_k\}$
15: **else**
16:      $a_l \leftarrow a_l \cup \{c_k\}$
17:      Calculate $\Delta(c_k)$ according to Equation (6.3)
18:      **if** $\Delta(c_k) \leq \gamma$ **then**
19:          $\mathcal{E} \leftarrow \mathcal{E} \cup \{c_k\}$
20:      **else**
21:          $\mathcal{E}_l \leftarrow \{c_j | c_j \in \mathcal{E} \wedge c_j \cap c_k \neq \emptyset\}$
22:          **for all** $c_j \in \mathcal{E}_l$ **do**
23:              Remove c_j from training set $\mathcal{A}$
24:              Reclassify c_j
25:              **if** $\Delta(c_j) > \gamma$ **then**
26:                  $\mathcal{E} \leftarrow \mathcal{E} - \{c_j\}$
27:                  Search for clusters fragments
28:              **end if**
29:          **end for**
30:          **for all** $a_j \in \mathcal{G}$ **do**
31:              Calculate the similarity between a_l and a_j according to Equation (6.4)
32:              **if** $sim(a_l, a_j) > \gamma$ **then**
33:                  $a_l \leftarrow a_l \cup a_j$
34:                  $\mathcal{A} \leftarrow \mathcal{A} - \{a_j\}$
35:              **end if**
36:          **end for**
37:      **end if**
38: **end if**

6.2.2   SELECTION OF CANDIDATE CLUSTERS

Given a new citation record c_k with an ambiguous author name c_k^a, the first step of INC consists in selecting, from a set $\mathcal{A}$, the clusters that have at least one compatible name with c_k^a by using a specialized pattern matching function for persons' names (Lines 2–9 of Algorithm 6.12), which is based on the Fragment Comparison algorithm described in the Appendix A. Notice that this step avoids the need for comparing the newly inserted authorship record with all clusters in the training set, thus contributing to maintain the clusters' purity.

6.2.3 ESTIMATION OF THE SIMILARITY BETWEEN AN AUTHORSHIP RECORD AND A CANDIDATE CLUSTER

For each candidate cluster a_j (Line 4 in Algorithm 6.12), the similarity between the authorship record c_k and the cluster a_j that represents an author is calculated using a variation of the function proposed by Santana et al. [2015], as shown in Equation (6.1). Such a function consists of a weighted sum of the similarities produced considering each attribute in isolation.

$$sim\left(c_k, a_j\right) = w_a d\left(c_k^a, a_j\right) + w_c d\left(c_k^c, a_j\right) + w_t d\left(c_k^t, a_j\right) + w_v d\left(c_k^v, a_j\right). \quad (6.1)$$

The similarity function for comparing the attributes is defined as:

$$d\left(c_k^x, a_j\right) = \sum_{t_i \in c_k^x \cap a_j^x} w\left(t_i, a_j\right), \quad (6.2)$$

where

$$w\left(t_i, a_j\right) = \begin{cases} \left(1 + \dfrac{1 - n_i}{n}\right) \sqrt{\left(\dfrac{f_{i,j}^2 + 1}{|a_j| f_i + 2}\right)} & \text{if } n_i > 0 \\ 0 & \text{otherwise.} \end{cases}$$

Function $w(t_i, a_j)$ weights the terms of each authorship record, returning a value between 0 and 1, defined according to the following problem-specific heuristics:

- The higher the number of author names that include a term t_i, the lower is its discriminative power. The sum $(1 + (1 - n_i)/n)$ returns 1 if the terms are used only in one group or $1/n$ if the terms have been used in all groups.

- Given the occurrence of a term t_i, the value of the conditional probability $P(a_j|t_i)$ provides some evidence of the strength of the association between the authorship record that possesses the term t_i and the author a_j. Such a probability may be estimated by the fraction $f_{i,j}/f_i$, where, f_i is the number of citation records having the term t_i and $f_{i,j}$ is the number of authorship records in group a_j having the term t_i. However, this estimation may be biased due to the high imbalance commonly found in training data for disambiguation tasks. It is well know that publication patterns have a very skewed distribution (few authors publish a lot while most authors have smaller figures). To consider and reduce this possible bias, we multiplied this estimate by the distribution of terms in the group, given by the fraction $f_{i,j}/|a_j|$.

- In a incremental disambiguation task, the training data can be initially empty and then grows as new authorship records are classified. To smooth the value of the estimates described before, INC added the constants (1 and 2) to the quotient calculus along with the square root of the resulting value.

6.2.4   UPDATING THE TRAINING SET

Two specific issues that must be addressed when disambiguating author names in real-world collections are: (a) capability to treat "new" ambiguous authors, i.e., authors not previously known to a method, and (b) adaptability to changes in publication patterns. Thus, the last phase of INC uses the similarity values between an authorship record and groups of citations associated with authors in the training set to cope with both issues. Next, we detail the steps that automatically update the training set and define the cluster of an authorship record c_k.

Identification of New Authors.   A low similarity value between an authorship record and its most similar group in the training set may indicate the presence of a new author (i.e., an author not present in the current training data) or simply a shift of research interests of an existing author. Thus, INC uses a threshold γ to help defining the probability of finding a new author and to control the amount of fragmentation inserted into the training data.

Let a_l be the cluster of authorship records with the highest similarity with a new authorship record c_k. If $sim(c_k, a_l) \leq \gamma$, then a new cluster is created (Lines 11–13 in Algorithm 6.12); otherwise, there is enough evidence to include this new authorship record in the cluster a_l. This threshold also helps to control the purity of the clusters as it introduces a minimal requirement for performing an actual author assignment.

Updating Doubtful Citations.   As new pieces of evidence are included in the training set, it is possible to use the most reliable predictions to reclassify doubtful ones and, possibly, correct previous misclassifications. In this step, after defined the cluster of an authorship record c_k, all authorship records included in the doubtful citation set $\mathcal{E}$ that share at least one term with this authorship record are analyzed again (Lines 21–29 in Algorithm 6.12). To determine if a prediction is reliable or not, we use a confidence metric based on the values of the similarities between c_k and each selected cluster in $\mathcal{A}$, which is given by:

$$\Delta(c_k) = \frac{sim(c_k, a_l)^2 - sim(c_k, a_m)^2}{\sum_{a_i \in \mathcal{A}} sim(c_k, a_i)}, \tag{6.3}$$

where a_l and a_m represent, respectively, the first and second most similar clusters with respect to c_k.

This metric combines the information regarding how close c_k is to a_l and how distant it is from the other clusters, especially from the second most similar one. Given a limit $\Delta_{\min}$, the assignments with $\Delta(c_k) \leq \Delta_{\min}$ cannot be considered confident enough, so they are included in $\mathcal{E}$ for future revaluation (Lines 14 and 19 in Algorithm 6.12). Every time a doubtful authorship record c_j is reclassified, a new $\Delta(c_j)$ is computed in order to determine whether it must remain in the set $\mathcal{E}$ (Line 25 in Algorithm 6.12).

The $\Delta(c_k)$ value is limited by the value of $sim(c_k, a_l)$. When $sim(c_k, a_l) \leq \gamma$, a new cluster is created due to lack of evidence, so it is natural that $\Delta_{\min}$ be greater or equal than γ. Since Equation (6.3) tends to return lower values as the number of cluster increases, setting $\Delta_{\min}$ equal to γ can achieve a good balance between performance and accuracy, eliminating the need to set the value of an additional parameter. INC includes all test data (new authorship records) in the training set and uses the confidence metric only to determine which authorship records should be reclassified.

Identification of Fragmented Clusters. During the disambiguation process, the authorship record groups for authors who work in different research topics may be fragmented even using small values for the γ threshold. To alleviate this problem, every time a reliable authorship record is inserted into the training set, the similarities between the group assigned to c_k and all the other groups that have at least one term shared with c_k are calculated (Lines 27 and 30–37 in Algorithm 6.12). If such similarity is greater than γ these clusters are merged. Notice that in this procedure, we do not take into account manually labeled authors/groups, since we assume there are no doubts about the authorship of these citations.

For comparing two clusters we use the same model described by Equation (6.1), but with a slightly different similarity function to compare attributes:

$$sim\left(a_l, a_m\right) = w_a d\left(a_l^a, a_m^a\right) + w_c d\left(a_l^c, a_m^c\right) + w_t d\left(a_l^t, a_m^t\right) + w_v d\left(a_l^v, a_m^v\right), \qquad (6.4)$$

where $|a_l| < |a_m|$ and

$$d\left(a_l^x, a_m^x\right) = \frac{1}{|a_l|} \sum_{t_i \in a_l^x \cap a_m^x} w\left(t_i, a_m\right). \qquad (6.5)$$

This function gives the same results returned by the similarity function between an authorship record and an author when the cluster a_l has only one authorship record. This is important to keep coherence with the strategy used to identify new authors.

It is worth observing that the γ threshold controls: (i) the minimum similarity value between an authorship record and a group of authorship records needed to assign an authorship record to an author; (ii) the minimum similarity value between two clusters of authorship records to consider them as belonging to the same author; and (iii) the minimum value of Δ in order to consider an assignment reliable.

6.2.5 ESTIMATION OF PARAMETERS

INC has five parameters: w_a, w_c, w_t, w_v, and γ. The best values for these parameters may be obtained using standard procedures of cross-validation in the training set. In order to increase efficiency of this search, we list a few strategies, which are similar to the one proposed by Santana et al. [2015]. This process is performed in two steps in the following order: (1) definition of the values for weights w_a, w_c, w_t, and w_v; and (2) definition of the value for γ.

Attribute Weights. For an authorship record c_k to be correctly associated with an author a_l, the weights must be defined so that $sim(c_k, a_l) > sim(c_k, a_m)$, $\forall a_m \in A - \{a_l\}$. By using the training data (i.e., the data already disambiguated) it is possible to define a set of inequalities based on the difference of similarities between each attribute in the form $w_a diff_a + w_c diff_c + w_t diff_t + w_v diff_v > 0$, where $diff_x$ represents the difference $d\left(c_k^x, a_l\right) - d\left(c_k^x, a_m\right)$.

By using a cross-validation procedure in the training set, we obtain approximately $\bar{n}|\mathcal{D}|$ inequalities that compose a system, possibly unsolvable. However, the values of the calculated differences, i.e., $diff_a$, $diff_c$, $diff_t$, and $diff_v$ reflect the degree of importance of each attribute. For instance, if many authors publish in the same venues, some values of $diff_v$ will be very low (or negative) indicating that the weight w_v should not be higher than w_c or w_t.

Considering such observations, the adopted strategy for the definition of the attribute weights uses the negative differences of the similarities between each attribute x, obtained after a classification, as below:

$$diff\left(c_k^x, a_l, a_m\right) = \begin{cases} d\left(c_k^x, a_l\right) - d\left(c_k^x, a_m\right) & \text{if } d\left(c_k^x, a_l\right) < d\left(c_k^x, a_m\right) \\ 0 & \text{otherwise.} \end{cases}$$

For each authorship record c_k in the set $\mathcal{D}$, by using a 10-fold cross-validation, we calculate the values of $diff(c_k^x, a_l, a_m)$ for each attribute x and cluster $a_m \in \mathcal{A} - \{a_l\}$. The sum of these values are then normalized by using the equation below in order to define the attribute weights:

$$w_x = \frac{\max_i \log\left(-\sum_{c_k \in \mathcal{D}} \sum_{a_m \in \mathcal{A} - \{a_l\}} diff\left(c_k^i, a_l, a_m\right)\right)}{\log\left(-\sum_{c_k \in \mathcal{D}} \sum_{a_m \in \mathcal{A} - \{a_l\}} diff\left(c_k^x, a_l, a_m\right)\right)}.$$

Notice that this normalization ensures the minimum weight value equal to 1 to the least discriminative attribute.

Minimum Evidence.   The value for the γ parameter is calculated by maximizing the trade-off between the rate of correct assignments and the rate of identification of new authors. The higher the value of γ, the higher the chance of identifying new authors, with the downside of the possibility of increasing fragmentation in the final result. This trade-off may be represented as the following sum of probabilities:

$$\hat{p}(sim(c_k, a_m) < \gamma | a_l \notin \mathcal{A}) \hat{p}(a_l \notin \mathcal{A})$$
$$+ \hat{p}(sim(c_k, a_l) \geq \gamma | a_l \in \mathcal{A}) \hat{p}(a_l \in \mathcal{A}),$$

where c_k represents an authorship record, a_m the group with highest similarity with c_k and a_l the correct group of c_k. The probability that an authorship record belongs to an author absent in the training set, $\hat{p}(a_l \notin \mathcal{A})$, was manually set to 0.5. The conditional probabilities were estimated based on the following steps:

1. For each authorship record $c_k \in \mathcal{D}$ and author $a_j \in \mathcal{A}$, we calculate similarities $sim(c_k, a_j)$, not considering the presence of c_k in the training set; this is similar to a *leave-one-out* validation procedure.

2. For each authorship record $c_k \in \mathcal{D}$, we store in a set $\mathcal{F}$ the similarity value of the author's citation group, $sim(c_k, a_l)$.

3. For each authorship record $c_k \in \mathcal{D}$, we store in a set $\mathcal{G}$ the similarity value $\max_{i \in \mathcal{A}-\{a_l\}} sim(c_k, a_i)$, the highest obtained similarity not considering the similarity with the correct group a_l.

4. The set $\mathcal{F}$ is sorted in ascending order so that the positions of each value correspond to the number of authorship records with authors in the training set that would not be correctly assigned if the parameter γ was higher than $sim(c_k, a_l)$. These positions are used to estimate the probabilities $\hat{p}(sim(c_k, a_l) \geq \gamma | a_l \in \mathcal{A})$.

5. The set $\mathcal{G}$ is sorted in decreasing order so that the positions of each value correspond to the number of new authors that would not be identified if the value for γ was smaller than $sim(c_k, a_m)$. These positions are used to estimate the probabilities $\hat{p}(sim(c_k, a_l) < \gamma | a_l \notin \mathcal{A})$.

With the estimated probabilities, the final value for γ is defined as the one that maximizes the trade-off defined earlier. If the amount of training is very low, the value for γ may also be very low, therefore we empirically defined a minimum value for this parameter corresponding to the value of the lowest attribute weight. Using this limit, an authorship record that share only one term of the least discriminative attribute with the most similar cluster will always be assigned to a new author.[7]

6.2.6   DISCUSSION OF AN EXAMPLE

To illustrate how INC works, we consider the same authorship record and the same clusters shown in Figure 6.1. In addition, to simplify the discussion, let us take the ambiguous authorship record whose author is "Gupta, A.," represented by c_k. Clusters 1, 2, and 3 correspond to candidate clusters, represented by a_1, a_2, and a_3, respectively. Besides, to calculate the similarity between the authorship record c_k and each cluster a_j using Equation (6.1), we need to estimate the values of the parameters w_a, w_c, w_t, and w_v. However, as our example is very small, it is not possible to estimate such values and we just set them to 0.25.

Table 6.2 shows the values for $d(c_k^x, a_j)$ (Equation (6.2)), where $x \in \{a, c, t, v\}$ and $j \in \{1, 2, 3\}$. Notice that, considering the *author name* attribute, Clusters 1 and 3 have just one authorship record that shares the same value, whereas Cluster 2 has two. Thus, the similarity values for the *author name* attribute $(d(c_k^a, a_j))$ is greater for Cluster 2 (from author a_2) than for Clusters 1 and 3 (from authors a_1 and a_3, respectively). Considering the *coauthor name* attribute, "R. Bettati" published only two works associated with Cluster 2. Thus, the similarity values between the coauthor names from the authorship record c_k and those from the clusters a_1 and a_3 are equal to zero, and very high when compared with that from cluster a_2. The same

---

[7]Note that the value returned by the function $w(t_i, a_l)$ is never equal to 1 due to the presence of the constants 1 and 2.

Table 6.2: INC similarity values between the ambiguous authorship record and the clusters shown in Figure 6.1

Cluster	$d(c_k, a_j^a)$	$d(c_k, a_j^c)$	$d(c_k, a_j^t)$	$d(c_k, a_j^v)$	$sim(c_k, a_j)$
a_1	0.192	0.000	0.000	0.000	0.048
a_2	0.236	0.913	3.536	0.913	1.399
a_3	0.192	0.000	0.000	0.000	0.048

situation occurs with the *publication venue* attribute due to the term "system." For the *work title* attribute, c_k shares five terms with the second citation in Cluster 2, which rises the similarity between c_k and a_2 for the *work title* attribute.

Thus, with these similarity values, Cluster 2 will receive the authorship record c_k. Notice that this prediction is reliable because the $\Delta(c_k)$ value calculated using the two more likely clusters is very high, as shown below:

$$\Delta(c_k) = \frac{1.399^2 - 0.048^2}{0.048 + 1.399 + 0.048} = 1.308.$$

6.3 FINAL COMMENTS

Traditional author name disambiguation methods, like the ones described in the previous two chapters, usually perform offline to avoid damaging the contents of a bibliographic repository. Thus, they can spend a considerable processing time to disambiguate an entire repository. On the other hand, incremental methods are designed to perform on the online version of a bibliographic repository, which means that their complexity time must indicate a low processing time to avoid any additional impact to their users.

According to Esperidião et al. [2014], the time complexity of INDi, considering its merge-oriented approach MINDi (Algorithm 6.10), is $O(n_a + n_p + z)$, where n_a is the total number of identified authors in the repository, n_p is the size of the largest cluster of authorship records and z represents the cost to select representative authorship records from a cluster when comparing such clusters for reducing fragmentation. Notice that generally the number of authors in a bibliographic repository is much larger than the number of authorship records of a specific author.

Furthermore, even when the running time complexity to select representative authorship records is quadratic with respect to the number of authorship records in a cluster, it does not increase with the number of authorship records or authors in the bibliographic repository, but with the number of authorship records in that cluster. Thus, we may consider that the INDi complexity linearly depends only on the number n_a of authors in the repository. Moreover, the repository may be organized in ambiguous groups allowing one to compare a newly inserted authorship record only with those authors (clusters) from ambiguous groups whose names are similar to that of the authorship record being considered, which avoids a comparison with all authors and, therefore, considerably reduces the complexity of this task.

The time complexity of INC (Algorithm 6.12), according to Santana et al. [2017], is given by $O(|\mathcal{D}| + |\mathcal{A}||\mathcal{E}||\mathcal{V}|)$, i.e., it linearly depends on the size of the set of citation records ($|\mathcal{D}|$) in the training data (i.e., the actual bibliographic repository) and on the product of three terms: the number of clusters ($|\mathcal{A}|$) (i.e., the number of identified authors in the repository), the number of doubtful authorship records ($|\mathcal{E}|$) and the number of terms found in the authorship records belonging to a cluster ($|\mathcal{V}|$). Notice that, using proper data structures, like a hash table or an inverted list on the citation record terms, and applying a blocking strategy to group together all clusters with ambiguous authorship records would avoid comparing the newly inserted authorship records with all existing ones, thus considerably reducing the run time of INC.

We experimentally evaluated the disambiguation performance of INC, INDi and its merge-oriented version MINDi by using both real and synthetic datasets [Santana et al., 2017]. The real datasets considered in our experiments were KISTI-AD-E-01 and Cota-BDBComp, both described in the Appendix C, whereas the synthetic ones were generated by SyGAR. Regarding the experiments with real datasets and considering the K and pF1 metrics, INC obtained the best overall results followed by MINDi.

When considering the purity of the clusters given by the ACP and pP metrics, the best results were obtained by INDi, whereas in terms of cohesion, given by the AAP and pR metrics, INC outperformed INDi and MINDi. When using synthetic datasets for simulating the introduction of new authors, INC also outperformed INDi and MINDi in terms of the K and pF1 metrics. In scenarios simulating the change of the authors' research interests over time, INC also outperformed INDi and MINDi in terms of K and pF1, thus confirming its good performance in distinct scenarios.

CHAPTER 7

Additional Methods for Author Name Disambiguation

Due to the intrinsic difficulty of the author name ambiguity problem and the absence of a "silver bullet" solution, new methods are constantly being proposed in the literature. In this chapter, we briefly describe some alternative (recent) methods that follow specific approaches that might be considered complementary with respect to those presented in the previous chapters. We start by presenting in Section 7.1 a few specific author grouping methods that exploit graph-based representations. Next, in Section 7.2, we present two other author grouping methods that are based on new alternative predefined similarity functions. Our criteria of choice in these cases were diversity and recency. Then, in Section 7.3, we describe NameClarifier, a visualization tool for helping and guiding users in the author name disambiguation task. Finally, in Section 7.4, we address some recent approaches based on artificial neural networks, a trend in the area.

7.1 GRAPH-BASED AUTHOR GROUPING METHODS

Graph-based author grouping methods aim at solving the author name ambiguity problem by using a coauthorship network usually denoted by a graph $G = (V, E, W)$, where V is the set of vertices representing the authors, E is the set of edges representing the collaborative activities (coauthorship relations), and W is the set of weights w_{ij} associated with each edge $\{v_i, v_j\}$ [Han et al., 2011]. The weight of an edge is usually determined based on the frequency of the respective coauthorship, i.e., the number of articles published together or the number of authors on the articles. After constructing the network, graph-based author name grouping methods usually apply a graph clustering technique to gain insights about communities[1] of authors and patterns of collaboration. To run a graph-based clustering technique, we need specific similarity or distance metrics on vertices and edges.

The graph-based author name grouping methods, described next, attempt to find out communities in a graph by identifying hub vertices, i.e., vertices connecting such communities, and splitting them to solve the homonym problem, as shown in Figure 7.1. In such a graph, each vertex represents an author name ocurring in the authorship records and each edge a coauthorship relation. The vertex d, for instance, bridges two communities, indicating d as a possible homonym case, whereas vertex i is an outlier, i.e., a vertex weakly associated with a particular

---

[1]A community structure is a group of vertices in a graph that are more densely connected internally than with the rest of the graph [Xu et al., 2007].

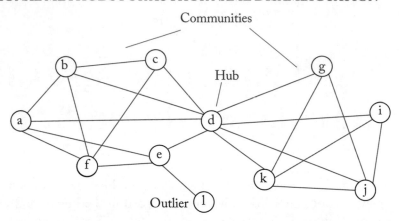

Figure 7.1: A graph G with two communities, and showing a hub vertex and an outlier.

cluster. Next, we describe some specific graph-based disambiguation methods that exploit such a representation.

GFAD (Graph Framework for Author Disambiguation) [Shin et al., 2014] addresses the author name disambiguation problem by merging and splitting vertices in a graph. By doing so, it addresses the homonym and the synomym problems altogether. Thus, given a set of citation records from a specific collection, GFAD constructs a graph $G = (V, E)$ following two steps. First, it creates a vertex $v \in V$ for representing an author (each author name corresponds to a vertex) and associates with this vertex an identifier, the author's name and her list of publications. Initially, all authorship records with the same name are associated with the same vertex. After this step, we have a vertex for each distinct author name from a collection. Then, considering each edge $(i, j) \in E$ as representing a coauthorship relation between two authors, GFAD adds an edge (i, j) to E if the authors associated with vertices i and j are coauthors of a same work.

GFAD's main hypothesis for the homonym problem relies on the fact that distinct authors usually belong to distinct communities during a same period of time. Accordingly, GFAD finds all non-overlapping cycles from a vertex in the graph to represent different author communities. For GFAD, vertices with distinct non-overlapping cycles correspond to authorship records from different authors with the same name. GFAD uses each longest cycle from a vertex v_i to split it into several vertices representing different authors. When splitting a vertex, GFAD also updates the list of authorship records and edges associated with each resulting vertex. For example, from the vertex d in Figure 7.1, we have two longest non-overlapping cycles, (d,k,i,j,g,d) and (d,c,b,a,f,e,d). Thus, GFAD will split d into two vertices, representing two different authors with the same author name. To solve the synonym subproblem, GFAD searches for vertices associated with similar author names by applying the longest common subsequence (LCS) algorithm [Bergroth et al., 2000]. It considers that two names are similar if the LCS result is greater than 0.8 (threshold empirically defined). If two vertices, with similar author names, are connected (directly or indirectly) through a common vertex, they are fused into a single vertex, updating its list of authorship records. To deal with authorship records without coauthors, GFAD first looks for their corresponding vertices. More specifically, let v_i be one of these vertices. GFAD looks for vertices whose associated authorship records have author names similar to those from v_i. Then, it selects the most similar vertex v_j, comparing titles from the authorship records associated with v_j and v_i, and fuses them.

LUCID, proposed by Hussain and Asghar [2017a], is a three-step graph-based author grouping method. The first step preprocesses the citation records to build a graph representing the coauthorship relations. Before building this graph, LUCID splits the authorship records (author names) into blocks (ambiguous groups) aiming to decrease the number of comparisons. LUCID also uses the Fragment Comparison algorithm proposed by Oliveira [2005] (see Appendix A), with its threshold value equals to 0.8, to group in the same block the authorship records with similar author names. In the LUCID graph, each vertex represents an author and edges represent the coauthorship relations between them. Initially, all authorship records with the same author name are associated with the same vertex. Thus, each vertex has an identifier, an author name and a list of authorship records associated with it. Considering Figure 7.1, each vertex is associated with a distinct author name and an edge (v_i, v_j) indicates that there exists a citation record that includes the author names associated with vertices v_i and v_j.

The second step focuses on the homonym problem and works along with the graph built in the first step. LUCID considers that different authors with homonym names should form different author communities. To detect such communities, it processes the graph using SCAN [Xu et al., 2007], a structural clustering algorithm for networks. SCAN receives as input a graph and produces as output clusters of vertices (communities), hub vertices, and outliers. For LUCID, each hub vertex represents a homonym case, i.e., it represents several authors, and then must be split into several vertices, one for each community.

LUCID's third step targets the synonym problem. For this, it searches for vertices associated with similar author names, using for this the Jaro–Winkler similarity function. In case the two vertices have similar names associated with them, LUCID fuses these two vertices if the geodesic distance[2] between them is smaller than three.

As an improved version of LUCID, in a subsequent work Hussain and Asghar [2018] proposed DISC (Disambiguating homonyms usIng graph Structural Clustering). In such a work, the authors use the *gSkeletonClu* algorithm [Huang et al., 2013] for identifying hubs, outliers, and clusters, instead of using SCAN. Following Hussain and Asghar [2017a], each hub vertex may represent several authors due to its relationshp with several communities (i.e., clusters). In addition, DISC splits a hub into two vertices whenever two clusters bridged by it have a Jaccard similarity below 0.2. This similarity value is estimated on the authorship records' work titles associated with the vertices in the clusters.

---

[2]A geodesic distance is the shortest distance between two vertices in a graph.

Finally, Gomide et al. [2017b] aim at solving the synonym problem by using only the structural information extracted from a coauthorship graph. Given a set of citation records C, a graph $G = (V, E)$ is constructed, where each vertex $v \in V$ corresponds to an author name (same author names from different citation records are represented by the same vertex) and each edge (v_i, v_j) represents a coauthorship. The problem addressed by this method is to determine a subset $S \in V$ that represents author names of the same author using no textual information from an author profile page (e.g., author profile pages from DBLP or Google Scholar). For this, the subset S must follow three properties:

1. S is a dominating set, i.e., a vertex $v_i \in V$ belongs to S or there exists an edge $(v_i, v_j) \in E$ and $v_j \in S$;

2. S is an independent set, i.e., for all $v_i, v_j \in S$, $(v_i, v_j) \in S$; and

3. If the number of vertices in S is greater than 1, for each vertex $v_i \in S$ there exist another vertex $v_j \in S$ such that the hop distance[3] between v_i and v_j is 2.

Thus, to find out the set S, this specific graph-based method starts with the set of candidate vertices $S_c = V$ and $S = \emptyset$, and performs the following steps:

1. Choose the vertex with the highest degree in S_c and include it into S, removing all its neighbors from S_c.

2. Choose a vertex from S_c that is at distance two from at least one of the vertices in S. If there is more than one option:

   (a) select the vertices with the largest degree;

   (b) from the vertices selected in (a), select those with more common neighbors with vertices already in S;

   (c) from the vertices selected in (b), select those whose edges have the highest sum of the weight $w2$ (defined next); and

   (d) from the vertices selected in (c), select those with the lowest sum of the weight $w3$ (defined next).

3. If more than one vertex remains after Step 2, stop returning the (incomplete) set S.

4. Repeat Steps 2 and 3 until S_c is empty and return S.

The weights $w2$ and $w3$ used above are calculated as follows:

$$w2_{i,j} = \sum_{k=1}^{|C|} \frac{1(l_i, l_j \in L_k)}{|L_k| - 1}$$

---

[3]The hop distance between two vertices is the size of the minimum path between two connected vertices.

$$w3_{i,j} = \sum_{k=1}^{|C|} \frac{1(l_i, l_j \in L_k)}{\binom{|L_k|}{2}},$$

where C is the set of citations and L_k is the set of author names in a citation c_k.

7.2   AUTHOR GROUPING METHODS BASED ON DISTINCT PREDEFINED SIMILARITY FUNCTIONS

There are heuristic-based domain-specific methods that exploit novel predefined similarity functions for solving the author name disambiguation problem. In other words, these methods group the authorship records belonging to a same author by using heuristics defined by specific similarity functions specially designed for comparing two authorship records. In this section, we briefly describe two specific examples of such methods.

DSHAC (DST-based Hierarchical Agglomerative Clustering), proposed by Wu et al. [2014], is a method that disambiguates a set of authorship records by following a hierarchical strategy. DSHAC first constructs seed clusters using the coauthor attributes. For this, it joins together in the same cluster authorship records that share at least two coauthor names. Next, in a iterative way, it calculates the pairwise correlations on clusters using an average-linkage criteria. DSHAC estimates specific disambiguation features from the authorship records by comparing their pairwise attribute values (e_1, e_2). For affiliation and publication venue attributes, DSHAC combines the Jaccard coefficient ($JC(e_1, e_2)$) and the Levenshtein distance ($LD(e_1, e_2)$) by multiplying them, for each pair of attribute values, $JC(e_1, e_2) \times LD(e_1, e_2)$, as feature values. For work and publication venue titles, the feature values result from applying the cosine similarity, the Jaccard coefficient or specific topic-based metrics on pairs of attribute values. For the coauthor attribute, a specific feature represents the total number of shared coauthor names. Another feature indicates whether the bibliographic reference lists from two authorship records share references in common. Finally, as a web-based correlation feature, DSHAC counts the number of times both authorship records co-occur in some of the authors' web pages (e.g., the author's Google Scholar page). DSHAC also uses the Dempster-Shafer theory [Dempster, 1967, Shafer, 1976] to fuse the disambiguation features and Shannon's entropy to estimate how such evidence is used to determine whether two clusters belong to the same author or not. DSHAC interactively fuses two clusters with the largest belief on combined pieces of evidence (if there exist ties, plausibility is used). It processes until a convergence test is satisfied.

Fast Multiple Clustering (FMC) [Liu et al., 2015] solves the homonym problem following a three-step approach. First, FMC groups authorship records with the same author name using the coauthor attribute, similarly as done by HHC (see Chapter 4). By representing the publications as a graph, each vertex corresponds to an article or a coauthor name, and each edge indicates a relation between an article and a coauthor name. If an article is reached by another article, both are put together in the same cluster. Then, using the title attribute, the most similar clusters are fused at each iteration until the highest similarity value among groups achieves a threshold value. The similarity between two groups is calculated by using the cosine similarity function, considering all publication titles together as a single document and weighting their terms by the respective term frequency. A threshold value θ is adjusted according to the number of publications that share a same author name following Equation (7.1), where $|S|$ is the number of publications with a given author name to be disambiguated, and α, β, and χ are three empirically defined hyperparameters. In their work, Liu et al. [2015] set the values of these parameters to 0.1, 0.3, and 200, respectively, by analyzing the results on publications with author names "David Brown," "Liping Wang," and "Wen Gao."

$$\theta = \alpha + \min\left(\left\lfloor \frac{|S|}{\chi} \right\rfloor \times 0.1, \beta\right) \tag{7.1}$$

Finally, the clusters are merged according to their respective venues. For this, a matrix $R_{m \times n}$ (*author* × *venue*) is built and then factorized into two other matrices, $W_{m \times k}$ and $H_{k \times n}$, such that $R_{m \times n} \approx W_{m \times k} \times H_{k \times n}$. In the factorized venue matrix $H_{k \times n}$, each venue has k features and $Q_{n \times n} = H_{k \times n}^T H_{k \times n}$ matrix representing the venue relationship. High values q_{ij} shows high relation between venues i and j. The matrix $R_{m \times n}$ comes from the top 5% full name authors with more collaborators in DBLP. For instance, the $R_{m \times n}$ matrix obtained by Liu et al. [2015] in their work was 2961×4772. The estimation of the similarity between two sets of venues, $V_1 = \{v_1, v_2, \cdots, v_m\}$ and $V_2 = \{v'_1, v'_2, \cdots, v'_n\}$, from two groups, is given by Equation (7.2).

$$Sim(V_1, V_2) = \frac{\sum_{i=1}^{m} \sum_{j=1}^{n} Q\left(v_i, V'_j\right)}{|V_1| \times |V_2|} \tag{7.2}$$

The venue similarity threshold value δ is also dynamically adjusted by Equation (7.3), where α, β, and χ values are empirically set to 0.2, 5, and 200, respectively.

$$\delta = \alpha + \min\left(\left\lfloor \frac{|S|}{\chi} \right\rfloor, \beta\right) \tag{7.3}$$

7.3   A VISUAL METHOD

Visual methods for author name disambiguation allow their users to interact during the disambiguation process, by confirming, rejecting, or indicating groups of authorship records that belong to a same author. An example of such a method is NameClarifier [Shen et al., 2017], a visual system proposed to interactively disambiguate author names from a collection of citation records. NameClarifier provides an interface that allows its users to visualize the similarity among author names already disambiguated in the collection and ambiguous ones.

As input, NameClarifier receives a set of authorship records that share the same author name. Three modules compose NameClarifier: *Pre-processor*, *Analyzer*, and *Visualizer* (see Figure 7.2). As can be seen, the *Pre-processor* summarizes the data from each authorship record in

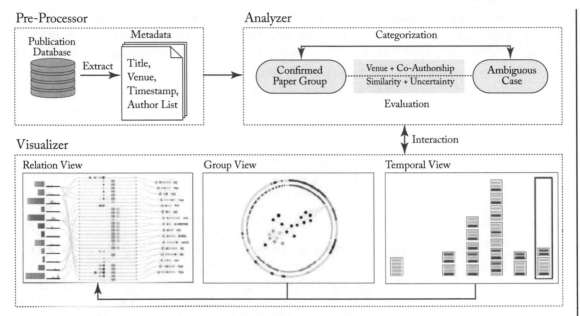

Figure 7.2: Overall architecture of NameClarifier (reproduced from Shen et al. [2017]).

five attributes commonly found in citation records: author and coauthor names, work title, publication venue title, and publication year. Then, the *Analyzer* receives the preprocessed records and interactively works with the Visualizer. Doing so, it splits the set of authorship records into two groups: the group of authorship records already disambiguated and confirmed, and the group of authorship records to be disambiguated, called ambiguous cases. Finally, the *Analyzer* estimates the similarities between the ambiguous authorship records and the clusters of disambiguated authorship records.

NameClarifier estimates the similarity between an ambiguous authorship record and a disambiguated cluster by using two metrics called *allocation likelihood* and *confidence*. The values of these two metrics are calculated for both coauthor names and publication venue titles. Allocation Likelihood ($AL(r, g)$) is the average of the estimated similarity values between an ambiguous authorship record r and each record belonging to a disambiguated cluster g. NameClarifier uses a weighted average of the similarity of the coauthor name lists (measured by the Jaccard coefficient) and the similarity of the publication venue titles of the two records (measured by $sgn(vs(v_r, v_i) - s)$, where v_r and v_i are the publication venue titles of the authorship records r and $r_i \in g$, vs is the Jaccard coefficient between the names of the authors that published in the venues entitled v_r and v_i, and $s = 0.1$ is a threshold value. The values 0.8 and 0.2 are used as weights for the similarities between coauthor name lists and between publication venue titles, respectively.

NameClarifier calculates the confidence of an allocation likelihood based on several confidence metrics for publication venue titles and coauthor names. For publication venue titles, it considers the proportion of authorship records in a disambiguated cluster that corresponds to publications from a specific venue v $(ad(v))$, the similarity between publication venue titles v_r and v_i $(sv(v_r, v_i))$ estimated by the number of author names in common between v_r and vi using the Jaccard coeficient, and the level of research interest of the publication venue $(\mathbb{1}_{vr}(v))$ that was manually estimated. In this case, $\mathbb{1}_{vr}(v) = 0$ means a publication venue v with focus on several research areas and $\mathbb{1}_{vr}(v) = 1$ means a publication venue v with focus on few research areas. Thus, *publication venue confidence* is defined as $vc(r_i, r) = \mathbb{1}_{vr}(v_i) \times (ad(v_i) + vs(v_i, v_r))$.

According to Shen et al. [2017], the *coauthor confidence* (cc) of a coauthor name c is given by Equation (7.4):

$$cc(c) = \mathbb{1}_{DC}(c) \times (cf(c) + gq(c)), \tag{7.4}$$

where $\mathbb{1}_{DC}(c)$ indicates whether a disambiguated cluster g and an authorship record r share the coauthor name c, $cf(c)$ is the collaboration frequency, i.e., the number of authorship records belonging to a disambiguated cluster g published by a coauthor name c, and $gq(c)$ is the group quality. $gq(c)$ uses the density of a coauthor and the publication venue graphs to estimate such a quality by a weighted average between them with the same weights used by Allocation Likelihood.

The *Visualizer* module includes three components: *Relation View*, *Group View*, and *Temporal View* (see Figure 7.2). The *Relation View* component allows one to visually compare the disambiguated clusters and the ambiguous authorship records by encoding their similarities and confidences. The *Group View* component helps to certificate the correct author, allowing the user to check distinct disambiguated clusters of a same author and authorship records erroneously assigned to a disambiguated cluster. The *Temporal View* component allows to compare an authorship record against its likely disambiguated clusters by means of temporal patterns of publications in the disambiguated clusters (a disambiguated cluster represents an author by means of her/his authorship records).

In addition, the *Relation View* component also allows the users to add an authorship record to a disambiguated cluster, whereas the *Group View* component assists the users to identify new authors and then create new disambiguated clusters, and correct erroneously assigned authorship records to a cluster. Any change performed using the *Visualizer* makes the *Analyzer* to recalculate similarities and confidence measures.

7.4 APPROACHES BASED ON ARTIFICIAL NEURAL NETWORKS

The popularity of Artificial Neural Networks (ANNs) in many applications in which they are currently the state-of-the-art, such as Computer Vision [Voulodimos et al., 2018] and Natural Language Processing [Devlin et al., 2018, Young et al., 2018], motivated the first attempts to exploit ANNs in the author name disambiguation problem. These attempts, although recent, are very simplistic and basically apply the ANNs as a supervised binary classifier for the author assignment sub-problem. Given two authorship records with ambiguous author names, the records are classified by the trained ANN as a match or non-match (same author or not).

ANNs are computer models designed to simulate the way the human brain processes information. ANNs, as most supervised methods, detect patterns and relationships among the input variables by learning from the (training) data. Generally speaking, an ANN is formed by several single units, called processing elements (PE) or artificial neurons, inter-connected with coefficients (weights), which constitute the neural structure, eventually organized into layers. The connections among the neural computations are what provide the flexibility of the ANNs, allowing its application and adaptation to many real-world problems.

Each PE in the network has weighted inputs, a transfer (or activation) function and one output. The behavior of a neural network is determined by the transfer/activation functions of its neurons, by the learning rule (e.g., the optimized objective function), and by the network architecture itself. The weights are the adjustable parameters. The weighted sum of the inputs constitutes the activation of the neuron. The activation signal is passed through the transfer function to produce a single output of the neuron. Transfer functions introduce nonlinearity to the network. During the training, the inter-unit connections are optimized in order to minimize the error, obtaining a gradual increment of its objective function, for instance, accuracy. Once the network is trained, it can predict the output of previously unseen/unknown cases.

A schematic example of such an ANN[4] is depicted in Figure 7.3, where an interconnected group of nodes, representing each an artificial neuron, is shown. The example shows the input (left), the output (right), and one hidden (center) layer. Each arrow represents a connection from the output of one artificial neuron to the input of another one. The input data of the problem are fed to the network. Each node receives inputs, from the previous layer, weights them on the basis of their importance, computes a weighted sum of the inputs, and, finally, adds up an additional input b called bias to properly tune its output value (for smoothing, for instance). The nonlinear activation function (typically a sigmoid or ReLU [Schifano et al., 2018]) is then applied to the weighted-sum in order to produce the output value, which is in turn fed to the next layer or becomes the result of the network. Given n input features and m output classifications, the linear combination of inputs of a neuron k is given by $u_k = \sum_{j=1}^{n} x_j \cdot w_{k_j}$, where x_j is the j_{th} feature of the input and w_k the weight vector of the neuron k, with w_{k_j} the j_{th} element of the vector w_k, and the output of neuron k is $y_k = f(u_k + b_k)$, with b_k the bias associated with the neuron k. f is the activation function, which, in case of a sigmoid, is given by $f(x) = \frac{1}{\epsilon^{-x}}$.

During the training, the weights are initialized to small random values and the bias to zero. Then each input from the training set is forwarded from one layer to the next one until it reaches the output layer. In this phase, the network computes the output o and the error e

---

[4]This particular architecture is called a fully connected Feed-Forward Multilayer Perceptron (MLP). The network is fully connected because all nodes receive input from all others (but itself). It is Feed-Forward because there is no input from the hidden layers "backward" into the learning process; the information is always passed forward.

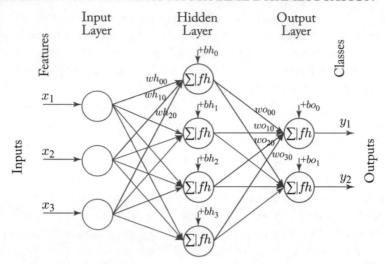

Figure 7.3: Example of an artificial neural network with input, output, and one hidden layer as described by Schifano et al. [2018].

corresponding to the input d.[5] The error e, calculated on a training or validation set, is then propagated backward changing the values of weights and bias in order to reduce the error itself.

Artificial neural networks can be trained using different approaches [Schifano et al., 2018]: (i) *online*, when inputs are processed sequentially, and weights and bias corrections are computed for each output; (ii) *batch*, when all inputs are processed in batch and correction happens only once; and (iii) *mini-batch*, when the training set is divided and processed in small batches, and the weight and bias correction is computed for each batch. An "epoch" defines when the entire dataset is processed forward and backward through the neural network. In order to reach high effectiveness, usually several epochs may be necessary to train the network in order to properly adjust the network parameters.

When used to solve the author name disambiguation problem, the input is usually the value of a similarity metric (e.g., cosine, Jaccard) applied to the attributes of two records (e.g., cosine distance of the corresponding titles), the weights in the hidden layers. The parameters of the architecture are learned from some training/validation set or adjusted empirically. The output is a final (usually softmax) layer that outputs the probability of match (same author) or *no-match*. The example in Figure 7.3 is exactly the Multilayer Perceptron (MLP) architecture proposed by Schifano et al. [2018]. They applied this MLP architecture, empirically tuned in a proprietary dataset and reported good results in terms of accuracy.

A similar architecture was proposed by Tran et al. [2014]. Their basic architecture is again a fully connected feed-forward MLP and the input layers are attribute-wise similarity measures.

---

[5]The output o and the error e are not shown in Figure 7.3.

The only difference is that it uses a so-called Deep Neural Network (DNN) architecture, which has basically more than one hidden layer. The idea is that the internal layers could somewhat learn more effective representations of the input features, especially targeted for the problem at hand during the learning process. In other words, there is an implicit internal "feature learning" during the ANN training. Results with a proprietary dataset report high accuracy values [Tran et al., 2014].

Kooli et al. [2018] were some of the first to test several different DNN architectures to the author name disambiguation problem. Although they tackle the general problem of entity resolution, they have tested a DNN architecture on author name disambiguation tasks, with a modeling very similar to the previous works in terms of input and output layers. More specifically, they tested with the traditional MLP architecture, but also with long-short term memory (LSTM) and convolutional neural networks (CNN). LSTMs were created to allow the network to maintain a memory of the previous inputs in a sequence, instead of using only the output of a previous layer as input to the next one. A CNN, on the other hand, has filters that continuously compact the input into more compact representations in each successive hidden layer. The idea is that the representations in the internal hidden layers can capture the most important aspects of the previous layer, preserving information and removing noise. In the comparative experiments, the CNN architecture produced the best results for the author name disambiguation task.

A very interesting approach is reported by Müller [2017], in which he uses three versions of an MLP for three types of authorship record: (i) Jaccard and cosine applied to normalized author names (called *simple coauthor model*); (ii) standard string similarity measures over the work titles (called *surface title model*); and (iii) a set of similarity metrics computed from a *word embedding* representation of the titles (called *semantic title model*). Each of these models is an MLP trained with a portion of the attributes, and each predicts a binary output (match or nonmatch). The binary output of the three networks are then combined by another MLP, *the joint model*, with a sigmoid activation function and a final softmax layer.

Besides the idea of combining the output of different models trained with different subsets of attributes, similarly to a multiview learning [Dalip et al., 2017], the most interesting aspect of this AND solution is the semantic title model that exploits word embeddings. The goal with the use of word embeddings is to capture semantic content similarity or relatedness between pairs of publication titles and author names, beyond surface-based string matching. The basic idea behind this strategy is that distributional (i.e., co-occurrence) information derived from a large text corpus can be captured and represented in a low dimensional vector space in such a way that proximity in this vector space correlates with semantic similarity or relatedness. Each word is represented in this space by a fixed-length vector and the closest the vector representations of two words are, the more semantically related they are.

Based on this property, it is possible to represent the work titles of two authorship records in this semantic model as the *average* vector of all words in the respective titles after stopword removal. The vector embeddings for each word were pre-computed in large external corpora including Glove (that uses Wikipedia) and DBLP. Experiments conducted with the KISTI-AD-E-01 dataset (see Appendix C) show a coverage (percentage of words in the KISTI-AD-E-01 dataset with pre-computed embeddings in the used corpora) between 80% and 90%, meaning that, on average, only 15% of the words occurring in titles of the KISTI-AD-E-01 dataset did not have a pre-computed word embedding. The best results were obtained with word embeddings extracted from DBLP, which makes sense since this is the corpora most similar to the KISTI-AD-E-01 dataset. Despite the good results obtained with this solution, they are comparatively worse than state-of-the-art author name disambiguation methods (e.g., the INC method, covered in Section 6.2) using the KISTI-AD-E-01 dataset.

Another interesting proposal is that by Zhang et al. [2018] that describes the author name disambiguation method applied in AMiner.[6] In their work, the authors propose a strategy for learning the representation of the authorship records and group them using a hierarchical clustering technique applied on their representations. Aiming to improve the disambiguation result, users' feedbacks are also inserted into the process. Such a method learns a global and a local representation for each authorship record. For the global representation, all authorship records are embedded into a unified continuous low-dimensional space. To this end, each authorship record is first represented by a weighted sum of its embedding features[7] obtained by using Word2vec [Mikolov et al., 2013]. Next, using triplets involving embedded authorship records with positive and negative examples, another embedding function is learned to get the final global embedding representations of the authorship records belonging to the same author. The idea is that records of the same author will have embedded representations close in the embedding space, while the ones belonging to different authors will be far away.

For learning a local representation for the authorship records in an ambiguous group, a graph is constructed, where each vertex represents an authorship record from this group and each edge captures the similarity between two authorship records that are above a given threshold. The similarity corresponds to the sum of the IDFs (inverted document frequencies) associated with the common features between two authorship records. Given this graph representation, a graph convolution network [Kipf and Welling, 2016] is used to refine the global representation with this graph-based representation. After obtaining the final refined embeddings, AMiner groups the authorship records belonging to the same author using a hierarchical agglomerative clustering technique applied to the embeddings. It also estimates the number of authors, i.e., the number of clusters, using a recurrent neural network for mapping the set of embedding vectors to the number of clusters in the set. To improve the results, AMiner allows its users to provide feedback for removing an authorship record from a cluster, adding an authorship record to a cluster, annotating a cluster that mixed authorship records, merging two split clusters of the same author, creating a cluster of authorship records and confirming that a cluster is cleaned.

---

[6]AMiner is the second-generation version of ArnetMiner [Tang et al., 2008].
[7]Here, each feature corresponds to a word in the work title or abstract, a coauthor or publication venue name, and an affiliation.

To summarize, some common aspects of these approaches show that they: (i) usually use only small datasets; (ii) are evaluated using basically accuracy, which may not be the ideal evaluation metric for the author name disambiguation problem; (iii) are not compared to state-of-the-art author name disambiguation methods, but only to traditional binary classifiers; and (iv) do not follow a rigorous scientific protocol that uses multiple datasets to ensure generality of the results, using multiple splits of the datasets into training, validation, and test to ensure low variability under different conditions, and applying standard statistical treatments to the results to reject the null hypothesis of equivalent results among the competitors.

7.5 FINAL COMMENTS

This chapter provided a glimpse on the new paths and venues that have been recently exploited for the author name disambiguation problem. As any exploratory task, it is not clear whether these endeavours will succeed in advancing the state-of-the-art in the field, either from a scientific or a practical point of view.

This is particularly evident in the case of the new ANN solutions, as it is still unclear the benefits of using such complex solutions for the author name disambiguation problem given that ANNs are: (i) very time consuming at training time; (ii) data-intensive in the sense that they require lots of data to properly work; and (iii) hard to assess due to their poor interpretability (i.e., they are hard to explain, particularly the cases of failure) caused mainly by model complexity and the huge amount of required parameters.

On the positive side, we would like to point out that lightweight approaches that extend or enhance the representation of citation records' attributes based on the word embedding vectors of selected words[8] have demonstrated potential in the AND task, even when using simpler classifiers [Kim et al., 2019b, Müller, 2017, Müller, 2018]. This so-called *embedding-based representations*, which are usually exploited along with other traditional (statistical) representations such as TF-IDF Bag of Words, not in substitution, are a promising alternative given the aforementioned drawbacks of applying a full ANN solution for the AND task.

---

[8]Attributes such as *work title* are usually represented with some type of pooling (e.g., average, max) of the embedding vectors of the individual words in the title. There are also reported cases when author names are represented as a pooling of embeddings of the name's characters [Foxcroft et al., 2019].

APPENDIX A

The Fragment Comparison Function

The Fragment Comparison is a simple, but very effective, pattern matching function for comparing proper names. It was proposed by Oliveira [2005] and has been used by several author name disambiguation methods, including those addressed in Chapters 4, 5, and 6, and by LU-CID [Hussain and Asghar, 2017a], briefly described in Chapter 7. Roughly speaking, this function checks whether two proper names are compatible by comparing their fragments based on the Levenshtein edit distance [Yujian and Bo, 2007] and on the matching of the initials of such fragments. A blank space between words in each string delimits the fragments considered.

Algorithm A.13 describes the Fragment Comparison function. It receives as input two strings, s_1 and s_2, and a threshold value lim, which is used by the Levenshtein edit distance to compare the two strings (names), returning *true* if they are compatible and *false* if they are not. Considering that a person name is minimally expressed by the initials of its first and last names, Lines 5–26 of Algorithm A.13 aim to reject comparisons between names obviously incompatible. Then, the following four loops (Lines 27–54) identify the similar fragments existing in both strings. The first loop (Lines 27–33) compares fragments including more than one character, whereas the following ones (Lines 34–54) compare fragments with only one character from a string with fragments from the other one. A final loop (Lines 55–63) then checks whether at least one string has all fragments marked. If this is true, the two strings are compatible and the function returns *true*; otherwise, the strings are considered not compatible and the function returns *false*.

As an example of how the Fragment Comparison function works, let us compare the names "Alok Gupta" and "A A Guta," using the threshold lim = 2, i.e., at most two character editions (insertions, deletions, or substitutions) are allowed to transform a string into another one. The Fragment Comparison function first compares the string "Alok" with the first letter of the string "A A Guta." As the string "Alok" begins with the letter "A", it then compares the last fragments from the two strings, "Gupta" and "Guta." Since the edit distance between these two fragments is equal to 1, i.e., it is smaller than the threshold lim = 2, then the function compares the additional fragments. In our example, only the second fragment "A" from the second name is not compared and, since the string "Alok Gupta" does not have an unmarked fragment to compare with "A", it remains unmarked. Once all fragments from the string "Alok Gupta" were successfully compared with the fragments from the string "A A Guta," the function returns *true*,

---

Algorithm A.13 Fragment Comparison (*Continues.*)

Require: Strings s_1 and s_2;
Require: A threshold value lim;
Ensure: A boolean value (Are c_1 and c_2 compatible?)

```
 1: c₁ ← s₁.split(" ")
 2: c₂ ← s₂.split(" ")
 3: n₁ ← number of c₁'s fragments (size of c₁)
 4: n₂ ← number of c₂'s fragments (size of c₂)
 5: if c₁[1].length > 1 and c₂[1].length > 1 then
 6:     if Levenshtein(c₁[1], c₂[1]) > lim then
 7:         Return False
 8:     end if
 9: else
10:     if c₁[1].length > 1 then
11:         if FirstCharacter(c₁[1]) ≠ c₂[1] then
12:             Return False
13:         end if
14:     else
15:         if c₁[1] ≠ FirstCharacter(c₂[1]) then
16:             Return False
17:         end if
18:     end if
19: end if
20: if c₁[n₁].length > 1 and c₂[n₂].length > 1 then
21:     if Levenshtein(c₁[n₁], c₂[n₂]) > lim then
22:         Return False
23:     end if
24: else
25:     Return False
26: end if

27: for i ← 2 to n₁ − 1 do
28:     for j ← 2 to n₂ − 1 do
29:         if c₁[i].length > 1 and c₂[j].length > 1 and Levenshtein(c₁[i], c₂[j]) < lim then
30:             Mark c₁[i] with c₂[j]
31:         end if
32:     end for
33: end for
34: for i ← 2 to n₁ − 1 do
35:     for j ← 2 to n₂ − 1 do
36:         if not marked(c₁[i]) and c₁[i].length > 1 and c₂[j].length = 1 and FirstCharacter(c₁[i])= c₂[j] then
37:             Mark c₁[i] with c₂[j]
38:         end if
39:     end for
40: end for
41: for i ← 2 to n₁ − 1 do
42:     for j ← 2 to n₂ − 1 do
43:         if c₁[i].length = 1 and not marked(c₂[j]) and c₂[j].length > 1 and c₁[i] = FirstCharacter(c₂[j]) then
44:             Mark c₁[i] with c₂[j]
45:         end if
46:     end for
47: end for
48: for i ← 2 to n₁ − 1 do
49:     for j ← 2 to n₂ − 1 do
50:         if not marked(c₁[i]) and not marked(c₂[j]) and c₁[i].length = 1 and c₂[j].length = 1 and c₁[i] = c₂[j] then
51:             Mark c₁[i] with c₂[j]
52:         end if
53:     end for
54: end for
```

Algorithm A.13 (*Continued.*) Fragment Comparison

```
55: for i ← 2 to n₁ − 1 do
56:     if not marked(c₁[i]) then
57:         for j ← 2 to n₂ − 1 do
58:             if not marked(c₂[j]) then
59:                 Return False
60:             end if
61:         end for
62:     end if
63: end for
64: Return True
```

thus considering the two strings, "Alok Gupta" and "A A Guta," compatible names under the threshold used ($lim = 2$).

APPENDIX B

SyGAR: A Synthetic Generator of Authorship Records

SyGAR is a tool for generating synthetic collections of citation records [Ferreira et al., 2009]. It was designed with the goal of creating synthetic datasets for evaluating author name disambiguation methods in more realistic, yet controlled, scenarios, such as those found in real evolving bibliographic repositories. For this, it captures aspects of real collections that are challenging to disambiguate and, therefore, to generate more appropriate synthetic collections to evaluate them. These synthetic collections may be larger and span longer periods of time, besides being representative of real data with respect to *author publication profiles* (defined below).

SyGAR takes as input a real collection of previously disambiguated authorship records, referred to as the *input collection*. Each one of such records is composed of the four attributes commonly exploited by existing disambiguation methods [Cota et al., 2010, Ferreira et al., 2014, 2010, Han et al., 2004, 2005a,b, Lee et al., 2005, Liu et al., 2015, Pereira et al., 2009, Santana et al., 2015, 2017, Shen et al., 2017, Shin et al., 2014, Zhang et al., 2019a], namely author name, list of coauthor names, list of unique terms present in the work title, and list of terms from the publication venue title. Authors with the same ambiguous name, and their corresponding records, are organized into *ambiguous groups* (e.g., all authors named "C. Chen"). SyGAR also takes as input several other parameters, defined in Table B.1 and described in the following sections, which are used in the data generation process.

As output, SyGAR produces a representative list of synthetically generated authorship records, referred to as the *output collection*. Each generated record consists of the four aforementioned attributes. In particular, the (synthetic) work title is represented by a set of unique terms as opposed to a complete semantically-sound sentence, as most disambiguation methods typically exploit the former.

The overall generation process consists of three main steps, as shown in Figure B.1. First, SyGAR summarizes the input collection into a set of attribute distributions that characterize the publication profiles of individual authors in the input collection and builds publication profiles for all authors and coauthors in the input collection. Then, the attribute distributions are used to generate synthetic authorship records (unless otherwise mentioned, only profiles of authors

Table B.1: SyGAR input parameters

Parameter	Description
N_{loads}	Number of loads to be synthesized
N_R	Total number of records to be generated per load
N_{Topics}	Number of topics
α_{Topic}	Threshold used to estimate distribution of topic popularity per citation (LDA model)
α_{Term}	Threshold used to estimate distribution of term popularity per topic (LDA model)
β_{Topic}	Minimum weight of the topics associated to an author
$\alpha_{NewCoauthor}$	Probability of selecting a *new* coauthor
$\alpha_{NewVenue}$	Probability of selecting a *new* venue
$\%_{NewAuthors}$	Percentage of new authors to be generated in each load
$\%_{InheritedTopics}$	Percentage of topics to be inherited from a new author's main coauthor
$\%_{ProfileChanges}$	Percentage of authors whose profiles will be changed in each load
δ	Shift parameter used to simulate changes in an author's profile
P^{FName}	Probability distribution of altering (removing, keeping, or retaining) only the initial of the author's first name
P^{MName}	Probability distribution of altering (removing, keeping, or retaining) only the initial of the author's middle name
$P^{LName}_{\sharp Mods}$	Probability distribution of the number of modifications in the author's last name
P^{LName}_{Mod}	Probabilities of inserting, deleting, or changing one character or swapping two characters of the author's last name
$P^{Title}_{\sharp Mods}$	Probability distribution of the number of modifications in the work title
P^{Title}_{Mod}	Probabilities of inserting, deleting, or changing one character or swapping two characters of the work title
$P^{Venue}_{\sharp Mods}$	Probability distribution of the number of modifications in the venue title
P^{Venue}_{Mod}	Probabilities of inserting, deleting, or changing one character or swapping two characters of the venue title

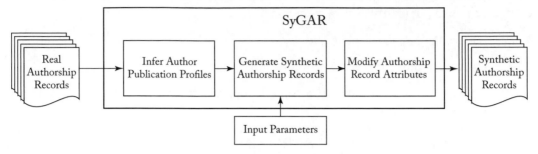

Figure B.1: SyGAR main components [Ferreira et al., 2009, 2012a]—SyGAR receives as input a disambiguated collection of citation records and builds publication profiles for all authors in that collection. Then, the publication profiles are used to generate synthetic authorship records. As a final step, SyGAR may introduce typographical errors in the output collection and change the citation attributes.

are used to generate synthetic data[1]). Finally, SyGAR modifies the authorship record attributes, particularly author names, in order to adhere them to a pre-defined format (e.g., keep only the initial of the first name). In this step, it may also introduce typographical errors in the *output collection*.

The following sections details how SyGAR infers publication profiles from the input collection (Section B.1), how it generates synthetic authorship records for authors already present in the input collection (Section B.2) and for new authors (Section B.3), how it models dynamic publication profiles (Section B.4) and, finally, how it modifies citation attributes (Section B.5).

B.1 INFERRING PUBLICATION PROFILES FROM THE INPUT COLLECTION

Each author's publication profile is characterized by her authorship records. That is, the profile of an author a is extracted from the input collection by summarizing her list of authorship records into four probability distributions, namely:

1. $P^a_{nCoauthors}$: a's distribution of the number of coauthors per record;

2. $P^a_{Coauthor}$: a's coauthor popularity distribution;

3. P^a_{nTerms}: a's distribution of number of terms in a work title; and

4. P^a_{Topic}: a's topic popularity distribution.

Each topic t is further characterized by two probability distributions:

---

[1]Profiles of coauthors are used in the generation of profiles of new authors (see Section B.3), which relies on the profiles of all authors and coauthors in the input collection.

1. P_{Term}^t: t's term popularity distribution; and

2. P_{Venue}^t: t's venue popularity distribution.

Finally, we also build a collection profile with:

1. $P_{nRecordsAuthors}^c$: probability distribution of the number of records per author with ambiguous names;

2. $P_{nRecordsAllAuthors}^c$: probability distribution of the number of records per author; and

3. $P_{nRecordsGroup}^c$: probability distribution of the number of records per ambiguous group.

$P_{nCoauthors}^a$, $P_{Coauthor}^a$, P_{nTerms}^a, $P_{nRecordsAuthors}^c$, and $P_{nRecordsAllAuthors}^c$ can be directly extracted from the input collection by aggregating the authorship records of each author a. We assume that a's attribute distributions are statistically independent. In particular, we assume that, for any given record, the coauthors of a are independently chosen. Despite somewhat simplistic, these independence assumptions have also been made by most work in the context of name disambiguation [Ferreira et al., 2014, Han et al., 2004, 2005a,b, Lee et al., 2005, Santana et al., 2017]. More importantly, Ferreira et al. [2012a] show that these assumptions have little (if any) impact on the performance of different disambiguation methods, as there is little difference in their results when applied to a real (input) collection and to synthetically generated (output) collections.

The main challenge here is to infer, from the input collection, the distributions of topic popularity for each author (P_{Topic}^a), as well as the distributions of term and venue popularity associated with each topic (P_{Term}^t and P_{Venue}^t). Recall that the input collection does not contain any information on the topic(s) associated with each authorship record. Thus, to address this challenge, SyGAR models each authorship record in the input collection as a finite mixture of a set of topics. In other words, each authorship record r has an associated *topic distribution* $P_{Topic}^r(t)$.[2] Terms in the work titles and the actual publication venue titles are drawn from corresponding distributions associated with the topics of the authorship record itself, and not with their authors. This model is thus able to generate an authorship record with a publication venue title and a work title containing terms not yet associated with any of their authors, provided that such terms and publication venues are associated with a topic of their interests.

A first step to infer P_{Topic}^a, P_{Term}^t, and P_{Venue}^t consists in deriving the distribution of topics for each authorship record r in the input collection, P_{Topic}^r. This is performed using the Latent Dirichlet Allocation (LDA) generative model, previously proposed for modeling document contents [Blei et al., 2003]. LDA is a three-level hierarchical Bayesian model, as illustrated in Figure B.2. In this model, ϕ denotes a matrix of topic distributions, with a multinomial distribution of N_{Terms} terms for each of the N_{Topics} topics, which is drawn independently from a

---

[2]$P_{Topic}^r(t)$ measures the strength at which a given topic t is related to the authorship record r, normalized so as to keep the summation over all topics equal to 1. Thus, $P_{Topic}^r(t)$ can be seen as a *weight* associated with a topic t for an authorship record r.

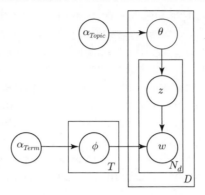

Figure B.2: A plate representation of the LDA [Blei et al., 2003]—The LDA model assumes that each authorship record r follows the generative process. r draws the number of terms N_d in the work title according to a given distribution, draws a topic distribution θ according to a Dirichlet distribution model with parameter α_{Topic} and, for each term, chooses a topic z following the multinomial distribution θ and a term w from a multinomial probability conditioned on the selected topic z, given by distribution ϕ, which in turn is drawn according to a Dirichlet distribution with parameter α_{Term}.

symmetric Dirichlet(α_{Term}) prior. N_{Terms} represents the total number of distinct terms in all work titles of the input collection, whereas N_{Topics} is the total number of topics used to model the authorship records. Moreover, θ is the matrix of citation-specific weights for these N_{Topics} topics, each being drawn independently from a symmetric Dirichlet(α_{Topic}) prior. For each term, z denotes the topic responsible for generating that term, drawn from the θ distribution for that authorship record, and w is the term itself, drawn from the topic distribution ϕ corresponding to z. In other words, the LDA model assumes that each authorship record r follows the generative process described below:

1. Draw the number of terms $size_{Title}$ in the work title according to a given distribution, such as a Poisson distribution [Blei et al., 2003] or, in our case, the distribution of number of terms in a work title for a given author a, P^a_{nTerms};

2. Draw a topic distribution θ_r for authorship record r according to a Dirichlet distribution model with parameter α_{Topic};

3. For each term i, $i = 1 \ldots size_{Title}$, choose a topic z_i following the multinomial distribution θ_r and a term w_i from a multinomial probability conditioned on the selected topic z_i, given by a distribution ϕ_{z_i}, which in turn is drawn according to a Dirichlet distribution with parameter α_{Term}.

Thus, the LDA model has two sets of unknown parameters, namely, the topic distribution associated with each authorship record r, θ_r, and the term popularity distribution of each topic j, ϕ_j, as well as the latent variables z corresponding to the assignments of individual terms to topics. Several strategies can be adopted to estimate θ_r and ϕ_j. Following Rosen-Zvi et al. [2004] and Song et al. [2007], SyGAR uses the Gibbs sampling algorithm [Griffiths and Steyvers, 2004]. This algorithm aims at generating a sequence of samples from the joint probability distribution of two or more random variables with the purpose of, for instance, estimating the marginal distributions of one of the variables. The Gibbs sampling algorithm constructs a Markov chain that converges to the posterior distribution of z by generating random samples from the observed data, and then uses the results to infer the marginal distributions θ_r and ϕ_j. The transitions between states of the Markov chain result from repeatedly drawing the topic of the ith term, z_i, from its distribution conditioned on all other variables, that is:

$$P(z_i = j | w_i = m, z_{-i}, w_{-i}) \propto \frac{C^{WT}_{m_{-i}j} + \alpha_{Term}}{\sum_{m'} C^{WT}_{m'_{-i}j} + N_{Terms}\alpha_{Term}} \frac{C^{RT}_{r_{-i}j} + \alpha_{Topic}}{\sum_{j'} C^{RT}_{r_{-i}j'} + N_{Topics}\alpha_{Topic}}. \quad \text{(B.1)}$$

In other words, it computes the probability that the topic assigned to the ith term (variable z_i) is j, given that the ith term (variable w_i) is m and considering all topic assignments, except the one related to the ith term (z_{-i}). $C^{WT}_{m_{-i}j}$ is the number of times that a term m is assigned to a topic j excluding the current instance of the term m, $C^{WT}_{m'_{-i}j}$ is the number of times that all terms in the collection are assigned to topic j excluding the current instance of m, $C^{RT}_{r_{-i}j}$ is the number of times that the topic j is assigned to terms in the authorship record r excluding the current instance of m, and $C^{RT}_{r_{-i}j'}$ is the number of times that all topics are assigned to terms in the authorship record r excluding the current instance of m.

From any sample from this Markov chain, SyGAR estimates the probability of drawing a topic j for a citation r as

$$\theta_r(j) = \frac{C^{RT}_{rj} + \alpha_{Topic}}{\sum_{j'} C^{RT}_{rj'} + N_{Topics}\alpha_{Topic}} \quad \text{(B.2)}$$

and the probability of drawing a term m for a given topic j as

$$\phi_j(m) = \frac{C^{WT}_{mj} + \alpha_{Term}}{\sum_{m'} C^{WT}_{m'j} + N_{Terms}\alpha_{Term}}. \quad \text{(B.3)}$$

These distributions correspond to the predictive distributions over new terms and new topics. According to Blei et al. [2003], it is recommended to assign positive values to the input parameters α_{Topic} and α_{Term}, so as to allow the selection of new topics and new terms that have not been previously observed. In other words, positive values for these parameters ultimately imply in non-zero probabilities to all items (i.e., topics or terms) regardless of whether they have C^{RT}_{rj} (or C^{WT}_{mj}) equal to 0.

SyGAR follows the aforementioned procedure by processing all authorship records in the input collection, one at a time. It uses the terms in the work titles to estimate the conditioned probability given by Equation (B.1). After a number of iterations, it estimates the topic distribution of each authorship record r, P^r_{Topic} (given by θ_r in Equation (B.2)) and the term popularity distribution per topic t, P^t_{Term} (given by ϕ_j in Equation (B.3)).

Afterward, SyGAR infers the topic distribution P^a_{Topic} of each author a by combining the weights of the topics of all authorship records in which a is an author. Only topics with weights greater than or equal to β_{Topic} (input parameter) are selected from each authorship record of a, in order to avoid introducing topics of very little interest to a in P^a_{Topic}. SyGAR also infers the venue popularity distribution of each topic t, P^t_{Venue}, by combining the weights of t associated with authorship records containing the same publication venue, provided that t has the largest weight among all topics of the given authorship record, i.e., provided that t is the most related topic of the given authorship record.[3]

Given the author profiles, SyGAR is ready to generate the synthetic authorship records. It generates a number N_{loads} of batches of data representing a number of successive loads. For each load, it generates a number of records given by N_R or, alternatively, specified based on the distributions of the number of publications per author per load.

B.2   GENERATING SYNTHETIC RECORDS FOR EXISTING AUTHORS

Given a collection of authorship records, a synthetic record is generated as follows:

1. Select one of the authors of the collection according to the desired distribution of number of records per author. Let it be a.

2. Determine the number of coauthors according to $P^a_{nCoauthors}$. Let it be a_c.

3. Repeat a_c times:

    (a) with probability $1 - \alpha_{NewCoauthor}$, select one coauthor according to $P^a_{Coauthor}$;

    (b) otherwise, uniformly select a *new coauthor* among the remaining coauthors in the input collection.

4. Combine the topic distributions of a with each of the selected coauthors. Let it be P^{all}_{Topic}.

5. Select the number of terms in the title according to P^a_{nTerms}. Let it be a_t.

6. Repeat a_t times: select a topic t according to P^{all}_{Topic} and select a term for the work title according to P^t_{Term}.

7. Select the publication venue:

[3]These probabilities are combined by first summing up all values of $C^{RT}_{rj} + \alpha_{Topic}$ (numerator in Equation (B.2)) for authorship record r and topic of interest j, and then normalizing them so as to keep the total probability equal to 1.

(a) with probability $1 - \alpha_{NewVenue}$, select a venue according to P^t_{Venue}, where t is the topic that was selected most often in Step 6;

(b) otherwise, randomly select a *new venue* among the remaining venues in the input collection.

Step 1 uses either the collection profile, i.e., $P^c_{nRecordsAuthors}$, or a distribution specified as part of the input. The latter may be specified by, for instance, providing the fractions of records to be generated for each author. This alternative input adds flexibility to our tool as it allows one to experiment with various scenarios by generating synthetic collections with varying numbers of records per author profile. Steps 2 and 5 use the distributions in the profile of the selected author. The same holds for Steps 3 and 7, although, with probabilities $\alpha_{NewCoauthor}$ and $\alpha_{NewVenue}$, SyGAR selects new coauthors and new publication venues (i.e., coauthors and venues that are not associated with the selected author in the input collection), respectively. Also notice that, Steps 3 and 6 do not allow for a coauthor (or term) to be selected more than once.

The combined topic distribution P^{all}_{Topic} (Step 4) is obtained by first selecting only the topics that are shared by *all selected authors* (a and her coauthors). If there is no shared topic, we take the union of all topics associated with the selected author a and the coauthors. The combined distribution is built by, for each topic t, averaging $P^a_{Topic}(t)$ across all authors (a and the coauthors) and normalizing these values at the end so as to keep the summation over all topics equal to 1.

The seven steps are repeated a number of times equal to the target number of records in the new load.

B.3   ADDING NEW AUTHORS

SyGAR can also be used to generate authorship records for large author populations, by creating such records not only for the authors present in the input collection but also for new (non-existing) authors. A variety of mechanisms could be designed to build such records. For the sake of demonstrating SyGAR's flexibility, we adopted a strategy that exploits the publication profiles from author and coauthors extracted from the input collection.

A new author a is created by first selecting one of its coauthors among all authors in the input collection, i.e., using $P^c_{nRecordsAllAuthors}$. Let say it is c_a. The new author inherits c_a's profile, but the inherited topic and coauthor distributions are changed as follows. First, the new author inherits only a percentage $\%_{InheritedTopics}$ of the topics associated with c_a, i.e., the topics that are more strongly related to her (i.e., with largest weights). Let l_{Topic} be this list of inherited topics. The new author's topic popularity distribution is built by using the same weights c_a's distribution for the inherited topics, rescaling them afterward so as to keep the summation equal to 1.

Similarly, we set a's coauthor list equal to c_a plus all coauthors of c_a that have at least one of the topics in l_{Topic} associated with them. Once again, the probabilities of selecting each coauthor are also inherited, and rescaled afterward. However, we force that c_a appears in all records generated to the new author. This strategy mimics the case of a new author who, starting its publication career, follows part of the interests (topics) of one who will be a frequent coauthor (e.g., advisor or colleague).

Finally, the name of the new author is generated with the initial of the first name and the full last name of an existing author, selected from the input collection using the distribution of the number of records per ambiguous group, i.e., $P^c_{nRecordsGroup}$. A parameter $\%_{NewAuthors}$ specifies the percentage of new authors generated for each new load.

B.4   CHANGING AN AUTHOR'S PROFILE

SyGAR also allows one to experiment with dynamic author profiles, mimicking scenarios in which authors may change their publication profiles over time due to shifts in interests, as occurs in real-world bibliographic repositories. Although SyGAR processes the input collection as a static snapshot of publication profiles, the tool can generate collections in which authors dynamically change their attribute distributions over successive loads.

In the lack of a previous characterization of dynamic properties of author publication, SyGAR implements a simple strategy to change the *topic distribution* of an author a (illustrated in Figure B.3a). It first sorts the topics associated with a according to their probabilities (i.e., P^a_{Topic}), in order to have a histogram as close to a bell shape as possible (i.e., mode in the center and least probable topics in both extremes), as illustrated in Figure B.3b. It then shifts the distribution along the x-axis by a factor of δ, at each load. Figure B.3c illustrates four successive changes in an author's profile using δ equals to 5.

By carefully choosing δ, this procedure guarantees that changes occur as softly as desired, mimicking the case of an author smoothly increasing/decreasing her interest in some topics over time. Likewise, a parameter $\%_{ProfileChanges}$ specifies the percentage of authors that will experience changes in their profiles in each load.

B.5   MODIFYING CITATION ATTRIBUTES

The final step in the authorship record generation process consists of modifying the citation attributes according to several input probability distributions (see Table B.1). Two mandatory changes refer to how an author's first and middle names should be presented in the authorship record. There are three possibilities: completely remove the first/middle name, keep the first/middle name entirely, and keep only the initial of the first/middle name. Probability distributions P^{FName} and P^{MName} are used to make the selections, which are applied to the names of all authors and coauthors in the synthetic authorship records.

Next, six input distributions may be used to introduce typographical errors in the generated records. $P^{LName}_{\#Mods}$, $P^{Title}_{\#Mods}$, and $P^{Venue}_{\#Mods}$, are used to draw the number of modifications in each author's last name, work title and publication venue, respectively, whereas P^{LName}_{Mod}, P^{Title}_{Mod}, and P^{Venue}_{Mod} are used to draw the type of each such modification in each attribute. Four modifications

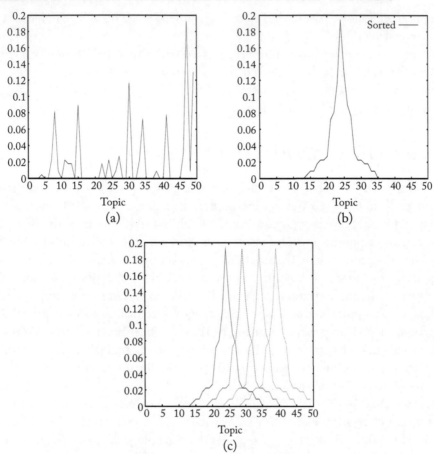

Figure B.3: Changing author a's profile by altering her topic distribution. (a) The original topic distribution of author a. (b) The topics associated with a sorted according to their probabilities (P_{Topic}^a) in order to have a histogram as close to a bell shape as possible. (c) The topic distribution shifted along the x-axis by a factor $\delta = 5$; 2 shifts are shown in the figure.

are possible, namely, insert, remove or change one character, and swap two randomly selected characters.

Finally, we emphasize that, although SyGAR was designed to help addressing the author name disambiguation task, it can be also used to generate any collection of authorship records, as long as a real collection is provided as source of author profiles. Thus, we believe it can be used to study other problems related to bibliographic repositories (e.g., scalability and performance issues). SyGAR has been implemented in Java and is available for download at http://www.lbd.dcc.ufmg.br/SyGAR.

APPENDIX C

Datasets

Among the bibliographic repositories more commonly used to produce datasets for evaluating author name disambiguation methods, we can mention CiteSeer, BDBComp, DBLP, and Rexa[1] that contain citation records of computer science publications, arXiv[2] that contains citation records from high physics publications, BioBase[3] that contains citation records from biological publications, and PubMed and BioMed that contain citation records from biomedical publications. In this appendix, we describe five datasets commonly used to evaluate author name disambiguation methods: Han-DBLP, Cota-DBLP, Cota-BDBComp, KISTI-AD-E-01, and SCAD-zbMATH. The first four of these datasets have been created from data extracted from two of the above listed bibliographic repositories, BDBComp and DBLP, whereas the last one is based on data extracted from a specific indexing and reviewing service. Some of these datasets were used in our experiments, whose results are briefly reported in Chapters 4, 5, and 6. For more details on other datasets refer, for instance, to Müller et al. [2017], who report on other datasets provided to assess the author name disambiguation task.

The Han-DBLP dataset was created by Han et al. [2004] from authorship records extracted from DBLP and manually labeled by them. For this, they used the authors' publication home pages, affiliation name, e-mail, and the names of their respective coauthors in full format. They also sent emails to some authors to confirm their respective authorships. Authorship records for which they had insufficient information to be properly assessed were discharged. This dataset contains 8,453 authorship records, with 480 distinct authors, divided into 14 ambiguous groups. Table C.1 shows the number of authors and authorship records in each ambiguous group of this dataset. The Cota-DBLP dataset is derived from the Han-DBLP [Cota et al., 2010]. It sums up 4,270 authorship records associated with 220 distinct authors, which means an average of approximately 20 authorship records per author. This dataset includes 2,267 authorship records whose author names are in short format, as shown in Table C.2.

Cota et al. [2010] also extracted authorship records from BDBComp providing the Cota-BDBComp dataset. This dataset sums up 361 authorship records associated with 205 distinct authors, approximately two authorship records per author, in which only eight author names are in short format. Although the Cota-BDBComp dataset is much smaller than the previous ones, it is very difficult to disambiguate because it includes many authors with only one authorship

---

[1]http://www.rexa.info/
[2]http://www.cs.cornell.edu/projects/kddcup
[3]http://www.elsevier.com/wps/find/bibliographicdatabasedescription.cws_home/600715/\description#description

Table C.1: The Han-DBLP dataset

Ambiguous Group	Number of Authors	Number of Records
A. Gupta	26	577
A. Kumar	14	244
C. Chen	61	800
D. Johnson	15	368
J. Lee	100	1,417
J. Martin	16	112
J. Robinson	12	171
J. Smith	31	927
K. Tanaka	10	280
M. Brown	13	153
M. Jones	13	259
M. Miller	12	412
S. Lee	86	1,458
Y. Chen	71	1,264

Table C.2: The Cota-DBLP dataset

Ambiguous Group	Number of Authors	Number of Records
A. Gupta	26	576
A. Kumar	14	243
C. Chen	60	798
D. Johnson	15	368
J. Martin	16	112
J. Robinson	12	171
J. Smith	29	904
K. Tanaka	10	280
M. Brown	13	153
M. Jones	13	260
M. Miller	12	405

record. This dataset contains the 10 largest ambiguous groups found in BDBComp at the time of its creation. Table C.3 provides more detailed information about its ambiguous groups.

KISTI-AD-E-01 is a dataset built at the Korea Institute of Science and Technology Information[4] [Kang et al., 2011] for English homonyms author name disambiguation. For building this dataset, their creators first identified the citation records of the top 1,000 most frequent author names from a late-2007 DBLP version. Then, for each author name found in such citation records, they created a specific authorship record. To disambiguate this dataset, their creators submitted to Google search engine a query composed of the surname of the author and the work title of each authorship record, aiming at finding the respective personal publication page. The first 20 web pages retrieved for each query were manually checked to identify the correct personal publication page for each authorship record. This identified page was then used to manually disambiguate that record, since such page contains data about that specific authorship record and belongs to the correct author. This dataset includes 37,613 citation records, 881 groups of same-name persons, and 6,921 authors. Since all author names are identified, the total number of authorship records is 41,674.

SCAD-zbMATH[5] is a dataset created by Müller et al. [2017], whose citation records and, consequently, the corresponding authorship records were collected from zbMATH,[6] an indexing and reviewing service that provides reviews and abstracts for articles in pure and applied mathematics. The authors first filtered the citation records whose authors were manually disambiguated in zbMATH. Due to restrictions for using the data and the applied selection criteria, such as a citation record must have at least one author with six or more name variants (synonym problem) or an author whose name is identical to other ones (homonym problem), the amount of citation records was reduced to 28,321, corresponding to 33,810 authorship records. The distribution of the citation records by language in this dataset is: English 65%, Russian 12%, French 9%, and German 8%. Besides, 41% of the authors in this dataset have only one authorship record. SCAD-zbMATH preserves the authors' order and names in the citation records, having all author names been properly identified, i.e., disambiguated with respect to each other.

Table C.4 shows the number of citation records, identified authorship records and distinct authors in each one of the surveyed datasets [Müller et al., 2017]. Tables C.5 and C.6 show the distribution of authors by number of authorship records and the distribution of authorship records by number of authors, respectively.

Finally, another interesting initiative is the Author-ity dataset [Torvik and Smalheiser, 2009], which was created from PubMed data and has been used in some works [Lerchenmueller and Sorenson, 2016, Liu et al., 2014]. Author-ity[7] provides a platform that displays clusters of authorship records written by a same author and ranks authorship records similar to a given one [Torvik et al., 2005, Torvik and Smalheiser, 2009].

---

[4] http://www.kisti.re.kr
[5] Available at https://doi.org/10.5281/zenodo.161333
[6] https://zbmath.org
[7] Available at https://databank.illinois.edu/datasets/IDB-4222651

Table C.3: The Cota-BDBComp dataset

Ambiguous Group	Number of Authors	Number of Records
A. Oliveira	20	52
A. Silva	38	64
F. Silva	22	27
J. Oliveira	22	48
J. Silva	18	35
J. Souza	12	34
L. Silva	18	33
M. Silva	16	21
R. Santos	17	20
R. Silva	22	27

Table C.4: Dataset statistics

Dataset	Number of Citation Records	Number of Identified Authorship Records	Number of Authors
Han-DBLP	8,453	8,431	479
Cota-DBLP	4,270	4,270	220
Cota-BDBComp	361	361	205
SCAD-zbMATH	28,321	33,810	2,946
KISTI-AD-E-01	37,613	41,674	6,921

Table C.5: Publications per author. Identified authors with n authorship records [Müller et al., 2017].

| Dataset | Number of Publications | | | | | | | | | | | |
	1	2	3	4	5	6	7	8	9	10	>10	$\sum$
Han-DBLP	0	66	99	39	36	17	16	17	9	5	175	479
	0	14	21	8	8	4	3	4	2	1	37	100
Cota-DBLP	2	33	33	20	16	6	7	13	6	1	83	220
	1	15	15	9	7	3	3	6	3	0	38	100
Cota-BDBComp	151	35	5	3	1	1	2	0	1	0	6	205
	74	17	2	1	0	0	1	0	0	0	3	100
SCAD-zbMAT	1,198	414	223	166	110	76	68	46	41	32	572	2,946
	41	14	8	6	4	3	2	2	1	1	19	100
KISTI-AD-E-01	2,864	1,071	655	461	317	215	168	136	116	91	827	6,921
	41	15	9	7	5	3	2	2	2	1	12	100

Table C.6: Authors per publications. Publications with n authors [Müller et al., 2017].

| Dataset | Number of Authors | | | | | | | | | | | |
	1	2	3	4	5	6	7	8	9	10	>10	$\sum$
Han-DBLP	675	2,410	2,537	1,462	697	312	164	77	40	20	59	8,453
	8	29	30	17	8	4	2	1	0	0	1	100
Cota-DBLP	622	1,476	1,117	536	221	136	64	44	22	9	23	4,270
	15	34	26	12	5	3	2	1	1	0	1	100
Cota-BDBComp	11	104	95	75	37	25	5	7	1	0	1	361
	3	29	26	21	10	7	1	2	0	0	0	100
SCAD-zbMAT	23,409	4,400	461	44	1	5	1	0	0	0	0	28,321
	83	16	2	0	0	0	0	0	0	0	0	100
KISTI-AD-E-01	3,349	11,694	11,268	6,304	2,738	1,117	482	238	124	91	208	37,613
	9	31	30	17	7	3	1	1	0	0	1	100

Bibliography

Abdulhayoglu, M. A. and Thijs, B. (2017). Use of ResearchGate and Google CSE for author name disambiguation. *Scientometrics*, 111(3):1965–1985. DOI: 10.1007/s11192-017-2341-y 32

Agrawal, R., Imielinski, T., and Swami, A. (1993). Mining association rules between sets of items in large databases. In *Proc. of the ACM SIGMOD International Conference on Management of Data*, pages 207–216, Washington, DC. DOI: 10.1145/170035.170072 53

Artiles, J., Borthwick, A., Gonzalo, J., Sekine, S., and Amigó, E. (2010). WePS-3 evaluation campaign: Overview of the web people search clustering and attribute extraction tasks. In *CLEF LABs and Workshops, Notebook Papers*, Padua, Italy. 15

Backes, T. (2018). The impact of name-matching and blocking on author disambiguation. In *Proc. of the 27th ACM International Conference on Information and Knowledge Management*, pages 803–812, Torino, Italy. DOI: 10.1145/3269206.3271699 12, 21

Bagga, A. and Baldwin, B. (1998). Algorithms for scoring coreference chains. In *Proc. of the 7th Message Understanding Conference*, pages 563–566, Fairfax, VA. 15

Bergroth, L., Hakonen, H., and Raita, T. (2000). A survey of longest common subsequence algorithms. In *Proc. of the 7th International Symposium on String Processing and Information Retrieval*, pages 39–48, A Curuña, Spain. DOI: 10.1109/spire.2000.878178 78

Bhattacharya, I. and Getoor, L. (2006). A latent Dirichlet model for unsupervised entity resolution. In *Proc. of the 6th SIAM International Conference on Data Mining*, pages 47–58, Bethesda, MD. DOI: 10.1137/1.9781611972764.5 28

Bhattacharya, I. and Getoor, L. (2007). Collective entity resolution in relational data. *ACM Transactions on Knowledge Discovery from Data*, 1(1). DOI: 10.1145/1217299.1217304 21, 23, 25

Blei, D. M., Ng, A. Y., and Jordan, M. I. (2003). Latent Dirichlet allocation. *Journal of Machine Learning Research*, 3:993–1022. 32, 98, 99, 100

Cohen, W. W., Ravikumar, P. D., and Fienberg, S. E. (2003). A comparison of string distance metrics for name-matching tasks. In *Proc. of the IJCAI-03 Workshop on Information Integration on the Web*, pages 73–78, Acapulco, Mexico. 24

Cota, R. G., Ferreira, A. A., Gonçalves, M. A., Laender, A. H. F., and Nascimento, C. (2010). An unsupervised heuristic-based hierarchical method for name disambiguation in bibliographic citations. *Journal of the American Society for Information Science and Technology*, 61(9):1853–1870. DOI: 10.1002/asi.21363 14, 21, 23, 33, 36, 37, 38, 39, 44, 61, 95, 105

Culotta, A., Kanani, P., Hall, R., Wick, M., and McCallum, A. (2007). Author disambiguation using error-driven machine learning with a ranking loss function. In *Proc. of the International Workshop on Information Integration on the Web*, pages 32–37, Vancouver, Canada. 6, 23

Dalip, D. H., Gonçalves, M. A., Cristo, M., and Calado, P. (2017). A general multi-view framework for assessing the quality of collaboratively created content on web 2.0. *Journal of the American Society for Information Science and Technology*, 68(2):286–308. DOI: 10.1002/asi.23650 87

D'Angelo, C. A. and van Eck, N. J. (2020). Collecting large-scale publication data at the level of individual researchers: A practical proposal for author name disambiguation. *Scientometrics*, 123:883–907. DOI: 10.1007/s11192-020-03410-y 21, 23

de Carvalho, A. P., Ferreira, A. A., Laender, A. H. F., and Gonçalves, M. A. (2011). Incremental unsupervised name disambiguation in cleaned digital libraries. *Journal of Information and Data Management*, 2(3):289–304. 5, 14, 21, 59, 60, 66

Delgado, A. D., Martínez, R., Montalvo, S., and Fresno, V. (2017). Person name disambiguation in the Web using adaptive threshold clustering. *Journal of the Association for Information Science and Technology*, 68(7):1751–1762. DOI: 10.1002/asi.23810 23

Delgado, A. D., Montalvo, S., Martínez-Unanue, R., and Fresno, V. (2018). A survey of person name disambiguation on the Web. *IEEE Access*, 6:59496–59514. DOI: 10.1109/access.2018.2874891 23

Dempster, A. (1967). Upper and lower probabilities induced by a multivalued mapping. *The Annals of Mathematical Statistics*, 38(2):325–339. DOI: 10.1214/aoms/1177698950 81

Dempster, A., Laird, N., Rubin, D., et al. (1977). Maximum likelihood from incomplete data via the EM algorithm. *Journal of the Royal Statistical Society. Series B (Methodological)*, 39(1):1–38. DOI: 10.1111/j.2517-6161.1977.tb01600.x 31

Devlin, J., Chang, M., Lee, K., and Toutanova, K. (2018). BERT: Pre-training of deep bidirectional transformers for language understanding. *CoRR*, abs/1810.04805. DOI: 10.18653/v1/N19-1423 84

Diehl, C. P., Getoor, L., and Namata, G. (2006). Name reference resolution in organizational email archives. In *Proc. of the SIAM International Conference on Data Mining*, pages 70–91, Bethesda, MD. DOI: 10.1137/1.9781611972764.7 23

Esperidião, L. V. B., Ferreira, A. A., Laender, A. H. F., Gonçalves, M. A., Gomes, D. M., Tavares, A. I., and de Assis, G. T. (2014). Reducing fragmentation in incremental author name disambiguation. *Journal of Information and Data Management*, 5(3):293–307. 65, 67, 75

Fan, X., Wang, J., Pu, X., Zhou, L., and Lv, B. (2011). On graph-based name disambiguation. *ACM Journal of Data and Information Quality*, 2:10:1–10:23. DOI: 10.1145/1891879.1891883 23

Ferreira, A. A. (2012). Contributions for solving the author name ambiguity problem in bibliographic citations. Ph.D. thesis, Universidade Federal de Minas Gerais. 3

Ferreira, A. A., Gonçalves, M. A., Almeida, J. M., Laender, A. H. F., and Veloso, A. (2009). SyGAR—A synthetic data generator for evaluating name disambiguation methods. In *Proc. of the 13th European Conference on Digital Libraries*, pages 437–441, Corfu, Greece. DOI: 10.1007/978-3-642-04346-8_53 95, 97

Ferreira, A. A., Gonçalves, M. A., Almeida, J. M., Laender, A. H. F., and Veloso, A. (2012a). A tool for generating synthetic authorship records for evaluating author name disambiguation methods. *Information Sciences*, 206:42–62. DOI: 10.1016/j.ins.2012.04.022 6, 97, 98

Ferreira, A. A., Gonçalves, M. A., and Laender, A. H. F. (2012b). A brief survey of automatic methods for author name disambiguation. *SIGMOD Record*, 41(2):15–26. DOI: 10.1145/2350036.2350040 3, 21, 22, 30, 32

Ferreira, A. A., Silva, R., Gonçalves, M. A., Veloso, A., and Laender, A. H. F. (2012c). Active associative sampling for author name disambiguation. In *Proc. of the ACM/IEEE Joint Conference on Digital Libraries*, pages 175–184, Washington, DC. DOI: 10.1145/2232817.2232851 31

Ferreira, A. A., Veloso, A., Gonçalves, M. A., and Laender, A. H. F. (2014). Self-training author name disambiguation for information scarce scenarios. *Journal of the American Society for Information Science and Technology*, 65(6):1257–1278. DOI: 10.1002/asi.22992 6, 14, 22, 41, 46, 48, 49, 50, 56, 95, 98

Ferreira, A. A., Veloso, A., Gonçalves, M. A., and Laender, A. H. F. (2010). Effective self-training author name disambiguation in scholarly digital libraries. In *Proc. of the ACM/IEEE Joint Conference on Digital Libraries*, pages 39–48, Gold Coast, Queensland, Australia. DOI: 10.1145/1816123.1816130 22, 28, 95

Foxcroft, J., d'Alessandro, A., and Antonie, L. (2019). Name2Vec: Personal names embeddings. In Meurs, M. and Rudzicz, F., Eds., *Advances in Artificial Intelligence. Canadian AI 2019. Lecture Notes in Computer Science*, volume 11489, pages 201–213, Springer, Cham, Switzerland. DOI: 10.1007/978-3-030-18305-9_52 89

Franzoni, V., Lepri, M., Li, Y., and Milani, A. (2018). Efficient graph-based author disambiguation by topological similarity in DBLP. In *IEEE 1st International Conference on Artificial Intelligence and Knowledge Engineering*, pages 239–243, Laguna Hills, CA. DOI: 10.1109/aike.2018.00054 21, 23

Geisser, S. (1993). *Predictive Inference: An Introduction*. Chapman & Hall, New York. DOI: 10.1007/978-1-4899-4467-2 55

Gomaa, W. H. and Fahmy, A. A. (2013). A survey of text similarity approaches. *International Journal of Computer Applications*, 68(13):13–18. DOI: 10.5120/11638-7118 26

Gomide, J., Kling, H., and Figueiredo, D. (2017a). Name usage pattern in the synonym ambiguity problem in bibliographic data. *Scientometrics*, 112(2):747–766. DOI: 10.1007/s11192-017-2410-2 1

Gomide, J., Kling, H., and Figueiredo, D. R. (2017b). Consolidating identities of authors through egonet structure. In *Proc. of the ACM Web Science Conference*, pages 385–386, Troy, NY. DOI: 10.1145/3091478.3098862 80

Griffiths, T. and Steyvers, M. (2004). Finding scientific topics. *Proc. of the National Academy of Sciences*, 101(1):5228–5235. DOI: 10.1073/pnas.0307752101 31, 100

Gruenheid, A., Dong, X. L., and Srivastava, D. (2014). Incremental Record Linkage. *Proc. of VLDB*, 7(9):697–708. DOI: 10.14778/2732939.2732943 67

Haak, L. L., Fenner, M., Paglione, L., Pentz, E., and Ratner, H. (2012). ORCID: A system to uniquely identify researchers. *Learned Publishing*, 25(4):259–264. DOI: 10.1087/20120404 22

Han, D., Liu, S., Hu, Y., and Yongjiao Sun, B. W. (2015). Elm-based name disambiguation in bibliography. *World Wide Web*, 18(2):253–263. DOI: 10.1007/s11280-013-0226-4 6

Han, H., Lee Giles, C., Zha, H., Li, C., and Tsioutsiouliklis, K. (2004). Two supervised learning approaches for name disambiguation in author citations. In *Proc. of the 4th ACM/IEEE-CS Joint Conference on Digital Libraries*, pages 296–305, Tuscon, AZ. DOI: 10.1145/996350.996419 6, 28, 39, 56, 95, 98, 105

Han, H., Xu, W., Zha, H., and Lee Giles, C. (2005a). A hierarchical naive Bayes mixture model for name disambiguation in author citations. In *Proc. of the ACM Symposium on Applied Computing*, pages 1065–1069, Santa Fe, NM. DOI: 10.1145/1066677.1066920 22, 28, 95, 98

Han, H., Yao, C., Fu, Y., Yu, Y., Zhang, Y., and Xu, S. (2017). Semantic fingerprints-based author name disambiguation in Chinese documents. *Scientometrics*, 111(3):1879–1896. DOI: 10.1007/s11192-017-2338-6 31

Han, H., Zha, H., and Lee Giles, C. (2005b). Name disambiguation in author citations using a K-way spectral clustering method. In *Proc. of the 5th ACM/IEEE Joint Conference on Digital Libraries*, pages 334–343, Denver, CO. DOI: 10.1145/1065385.1065462 23, 28, 39, 56, 95, 98

Han, J., Kamber, M., and Pei, J. (2011). *Data Mining Concepts and Techniques*, 3rd ed., Morgan Kaufmann Publishers, San Francisco, CA. 26, 27, 28, 31, 77

Huang, J., Ertekin, S., and Lee Giles, C. (2006). Efficient name disambiguation for large-scale databases. In *Proc. of the European Conference on Principles and Practice of Knowledge Discovery in Databases*, pages 536–544, Berlin, Germany. DOI: 10.1007/11871637_53 6, 23, 27, 31, 39, 56

Huang, J., Sun, H., Song, Q., Deng, H., and Han, J. (2013). Revealing density-based clustering structure from the core-connected tree of a network. *IEEE Transactions on Knowledge and Data Engineering*, 25(8):1876–1889. DOI: 10.1109/tkde.2012.100 79

Hussain, I. and Asghar, S. (2017a). LUCID: Author name disambiguation using graph structural clustering. In *Proc. of the Intelligent Systems Conference (IntelliSys)*, pages 406–413, London, UK. DOI: 10.1109/intellisys.2017.8324326 21, 23, 28, 79, 91

Hussain, I. and Asghar, S. (2017b). A survey of author name disambiguation techniques: 2010–2016. *The Knowledge Engineering Review*, 32(e22). DOI: 10.1017/s0269888917000182 3, 30

Hussain, I. and Asghar, S. (2018). DISC: Disambiguating homonyms using graph structural clustering. *Journal of Information Science*, 44(6):830–847. DOI: 10.1177/0165551518761011 79

Jain, A. K., Murty, M. N., and Flynn, P. J. (1999). Data clustering: A review. *ACM Computing Surveys*, 31(3):264–323. DOI: 10.1145/331499.331504 49, 50

Kanani, P., McCallum, A., and Pal, C. (2007). Improving author coreference by resource-bounded information gathering from the Web. In *Proc. of the 20th International Joint Conference on Artificial Intelligence*, pages 429–434, Hyderabad, India. 26, 32

Kang, I.-S., Kim, P., Lee, S., Jung, H., and You, B.-J. (2011). Construction of a large-scale test set for author disambiguation. *Information Processing and Management*, 47:452–465. DOI: 10.1016/j.ipm.2010.10.001 107

Kang, I.-S., Na, S.-H., Lee, S., Jung, H., Kim, P., Sung, W.-K., and Lee, J.-H. (2009). On co-authorship for author disambiguation. *Information Processing and Management*, 45(1):84–97. DOI: 10.1016/j.ipm.2008.06.006 32

Kim, J. (2019). A fast and integrative algorithm for clustering performance evaluation in author name disambiguation. *Scientometrics*, 120(2):661–681. DOI: 10.1007/s11192-019-03143-7 13

Kim, J., Kim, J., and Owen-Smith, J. (2019a). Generating automatically labeled data for author name disambiguation: An iterative clustering method. *Scientometrics*, 118(1):253–280. DOI: 10.1007/s11192-018-2968-3 6

Kim, K., Khabsa, M., and Lee Giles, C. (2016). Inventor name disambiguation for a patent database using a random forest and DBSCAN. In *Proc. of the IEEE/ACM Joint Conference on Digital Libraries*, pages 269–270, Newark, NJ. DOI: 10.1145/2910896.2925465 6, 27

Kim, K., Rohatgi, S., and Lee Giles, C. (2019b). Hybrid deep pairwise classification for author name disambiguation. In *Proc. of the 28th ACM International Conference on Information and Knowledge Management*, Beijing, China. DOI: 10.1145/3357384.3358153 89

Kim, K., Sefid, A., Weinberg, B. A., and Giles, C. L. (2018). A web service for author name disambiguation in scholarly databases. In *Proc. of the IEEE International Conference on Web Services*, pages 265–273, San Francisco, CA. DOI: 10.1109/icws.2018.00041 23

Kipf, T. N. and Welling, M. (2016). Variational graph auto-encoders. *ArXiv Preprint ArXiv:1611.07308*. 88

Kooli, N., Allesiardo, R., and Pigneul, E. (2018). Deep learning based approach for entity resolution in databases. In Nguyen, N. T., Hoang, D. H., Hong, T.-P., Pham, H., and Trawiński, B., Eds., *Intelligent Information and Database Systems*, pages 3–12, Cham, Switzerland. Springer International Publishing. DOI: 10.1007/978-3-319-75420-8_1 6, 21, 87

Laender, A. H. F., Gonçalves, M. A., Cota, R. G., Ferreira, A. A., Santos, R. L. T., and Silva, A. J. C. (2008). Keeping a digital library clean: New solutions to old problems. In *Proc. of the ACM Symposium on Document Engineering*, pages 257–262, São Paulo, Brazil. DOI: 10.1145/1410140.1410195 1

Lagoze, C. and de Sompel, H. V. (2001). The open archives initiative: Building a low-barrier interoperability framework. In *Proc. of the 1st ACM/IEEE-CS Joint International Conference on Digital Libraries*, pages 54–62, Roanoke, VA. DOI: 10.1145/379437.379449 1

Lapidot, I. (2002). Self-organizing-maps with BIC for speaker clustering. *Technical Report*, IDIAP Research Institute, Martigny, Switzerland. 14

Lee, D., Kang, J., Mitra, P., Lee Giles, C., and On, B.-W. (2007). Are your citations clean? *Communications of the ACM*, 50(12):33–38. DOI: 10.1145/1323688.1323690 1

Lee, D., On, B.-W., Kang, J., and Park, S. (2005). Effective and scalable solutions for mixed and split citation problems in digital libraries. In *Proc. of the 2nd International Workshop on Information Quality in Information Systems*, pages 69–76, Baltimore, MA. DOI: 10.1145/1077501.1077514 95, 98

Lerchenmueller, M. J. and Sorenson, O. (2016). Author disambiguation in PubMed: Evidence on the precision and recall of author-ity among NIH-funded scientists. *PLoS One*, 11(7):e0158731. DOI: 10.1371/journal.pone.0158731 107

Levin, F. H. and Heuser, C. A. (2010). Evaluating the use of social networks in author name disambiguation in digital libraries. *Journal of Information and Data Management*, 1(2):183–197. 23, 26

Li, G.-C., Lai, R., D'Amour, A., Doolin, D. M., Sun, Y., Torvik, V. I., Yu, A. Z., and Fleming, L. (2014). Disambiguation and co-authorship networks of the U.S. patent inventor database (1975–2010). *Research Policy*, 43(6):941–955. DOI: 10.1016/j.respol.2014.01.012 6

Liu, W., Islamaj Doğan, R., Kim, S., Comeau, D. C., Kim, W., Yeganova, L., Lu, Z., and Wilbur, W. J. (2014). Author name disambiguation for PubMed. *Journal of the Association for Information Science and Technology*, 65(4):765–781. DOI: 10.1002/asi.23063 5, 107

Liu, Y., Li, W., Huang, Z., and Fang, Q. (2015). A fast method based on multiple clustering for name disambiguation in bibliographic citations. *Journal of the Association for Information Science and Technology*, 66(3):634–644. DOI: 10.1002/asi.23183 21, 23, 25, 27, 81, 82, 95

Louppe, G., Al-Natsheh, H. T., Susik, M., and Maguire, E. J. (2016). Ethnicity sensitive author disambiguation using semi-supervised learning. In Ngonga Ngomo, A.-C. and Křemen, P., Eds., *Knowledge Engineering and Semantic Web*, pages 272–287, Cham, Switzerland. Springer International Publishing. DOI: 10.1007/978-3-319-45880-9_21 23

Ma, X., Wang, R., and Zhang, Y. (2019). Author name disambiguation in heterogeneous academic networks. In *Proc. of the Web Information Systems and Applications*, pages 126–137, Cham. Springer International Publishing. DOI: 10.1007/978-3-030-30952-7_15 23

McKay, D., Sanchez, S., and Parker, R. (2010). What's my name again?: Sociotechnical considerations for author name management in research databases. In *Proc. of the 22nd Conference of the Computer-Human Interaction Special Interest Group of Australia on Computer-Human Interaction*, pages 240–247, Brisbane, Australia. DOI: 10.1145/1952222.1952274 1

Mikolov, T., Sutskever, I., Chen, K., Corrado, G. S., and Dean, J. (2013). Distributed representations of words and phrases and their compositionality. In *Advances in Neural Information Processing Systems 26*, pages 3111–3119, Curran Associates, Inc. 88

Milojevic, S. (2013). Accuracy of simple, initials-based methods for author name disambiguation. *Journal of Informetrics*, 7(4):767–773. DOI: 10.1016/j.joi.2013.06.006 21

Mondal, S. and Chandra, J. (2020). A graph combination with edge pruning-based approach for author name disambiguation. *Journal of the Association for Information Science and Technology*, 71(1):69–83. DOI: 10.1002/asi.24212 32

Müller, M.-C. (2017). Semantic author name disambiguation with word embeddings. In *Research and Advanced Technology for Digital Libraries—21st International Conference on Theory and Practice of Digital Libraries, TPDL, Proceedings*, Thessaloniki, Greece, September 18–21, 2017, volume 10450 of *Lecture Notes in Computer Science*, pages 300–311, Springer. DOI: 10.1007/978-3-319-67008-9_24 6, 21, 87, 89

Müller, M.-C. (2018). On the contribution of word-level semantics to practical author name disambiguation. In *Proc. of the 18th ACM/IEEE on Joint Conference on Digital Libraries*, pages 367–368, Fort Worth, TX. DOI: 10.1145/3197026.3203912 89

Müller, M.-C., Reitz, F., and Roy, N. (2017). Data sets for author name disambiguation: An empirical analysis and a new resource. *Scientometrics*, 111(3):1467–1500. DOI: 10.1007/s11192-017-2363-5 105, 107, 109

Oliveira, J. W. A. (2005). A strategy for removing ambiguity in the identification of the authorship of digital objects. Master's thesis, UFMG, Belo Horizonte, Brazil (in Portuguese). 25, 39, 46, 65, 79, 91

On, B.-W., Elmacioglu, E., Lee, D., Kang, J., and Pei, J. (2006). Improving grouped-entity resolution using quasi-cliques. In *Proc. of the 6th IEEE International Conference on Data Mining*, pages 1008–1015, Hong Kong, China. DOI: 10.1109/icdm.2006.85 23

On, B.-W. and Lee, D. (2007). Scalable name disambiguation using multi-level graph partition. In *Proc. of the 7th SIAM International Conference on Data Mining*, pages 575–580, Minneapolis, MN. DOI: 10.1137/1.9781611972771.64 23

On, B.-W., Lee, D., Kang, J., and Mitra, P. (2005). Comparative study of name disambiguation problem using a scalable blocking-based framework. In *Proc. of the 5th ACM/IEEE Joint Conference on Digital Libraries*, pages 344–353, Denver, CO. DOI: 10.1145/1065385.1065463 12, 34

On, B.-W., Lee, I., Choi, G. S., and Park, H.-S. (2014). Discriminative and deterministic approaches towards entity resolution. *Journal of Intelligent Information Systems*, 43(1):101–127. DOI: 10.1007/s10844-014-0308-5 23

Peng, L., Shen, S., Xu, J., Fu, Y., Li, D., and Jia, A. L. (2019). Diting: An author disambiguation method based on network representation learning. *IEEE Access*, 7:135539–135555. DOI: 10.1109/access.2019.2942477 21

Pereira, D. A., Ribeiro-Neto, B. A., Ziviani, N., Laender, A. H. F., Gonçalves, M. A., and Ferreira, A. A. (2009). Using web information for author name disambiguation. In *Proc. of the ACM/IEEE Joint Conference on Digital Libraries*, pages 49–58, Austin, TX. DOI: 10.1145/1555400.1555409 14, 21, 32, 95

Porter, M. F. (1980). An algorithm for suffix stripping. *Program*, 14(3):130–137. DOI: 10.1108/eb046814 34, 61

Rijsbergen, C. J. V. (1979). *Information Retrieval*, 2nd ed., Butterworths, London. 14

Rosen-Zvi, M., Griffiths, T. L., Steyvers, M., and Smyth, P. (2004). The author-topic model for authors and documents. In *Proc. of the Conference in Uncertainty in Artificial Intelligence*, pages 487–494, Banff, Canada. 100

Salton, G. M., Wong, A., and Yang, C. S. (1975). A vector space model for automatic indexing. *Communications of the ACM*, 18(11):613–620. DOI: 10.1145/361219.361220 39, 49, 65

Santana, A. F., Goncalves, M. A., Laender, A. H. F., and Ferreira, A. A. (2015). On the combination of domain-specific heuristics for author name disambiguation: The nearest cluster method. *International Journal on Digital Libraries*, 16(3-4):229–246. DOI: 10.1007/s00799-015-0158-y 6, 21, 23, 26, 27, 67, 70, 72, 95

Santana, A. F., Gonçalves, M. A., Laender, A. H. F., and Ferreira, A. A. (2017). Incremental author name disambiguation by exploiting domain-specific heuristics. *Journal of the Association for Information Science and Technology*, 68(4):931–945. DOI: 10.1002/asi.23726 5, 6, 14, 22, 59, 67, 76, 95, 98

Scheirer, W., Rocha, A., Sapkota, A., and Boult, T. (2013). Toward open set recognition. *IEEE Transactions on Pattern Analysis and Machine Intelligence*, 35(7):1757–1772. DOI: 10.1109/tpami.2012.256 5

Schifano, S. F., Sgarbanti, T., and Tomassetti, L. (2018). Authorship recognition and disambiguation of scientific papers using a neural networks approach. In *Proc. of the International Symposium on Grids and Clouds*, Taipei, Taiwan. DOI: 10.22323/1.327.0007 85, 86

Scoville, C. L., Johnson, E. D., and McConnell, A. L. (2003). When a rose is not a rose: The vagaries of author searching. *Medical Reference Services Quarterly*, 22(4):1–11. DOI: 10.1300/j115v22n04_01 22

Shafer, G. (1976). *A Mathematical Theory of Evidence*. Princeton University Press, Princeton, NJ. DOI: 10.2307/2529769 81

Shen, Q., Wu, T., Yang, H., Wu, Y., Qu, H., and Cui, W. (2017). Nameclarifier: A visual analytics system for author name disambiguation. *IEEE Transactions on Visualization and*

Computer Graphics, 23(1):141–150. DOI: 10.1109/tvcg.2016.2598465 21, 23, 25, 82, 83, 84, 95

Shin, D., Kim, T., Choi, J., and Kim, J. (2014). Author name disambiguation using a graph model with node splitting and merging based on bibliographic information. *Scientometrics*, 100(1):15–50. DOI: 10.1007/s11192-014-1289-4 14, 21, 23, 28, 78, 95

Shu, L., Long, B., and Meng, W. (2009). A latent topic model for complete entity resolution. In *Proc. of the IEEE International Conference on Data Engineering*, pages 880–891, Shanghai, China. DOI: 10.1109/icde.2009.29 32

Smalheiser, N. R. and Torvik, V. I. (2009). Author name disambiguation. *Annual Review of Information Science and Technology*, 43:287–313. DOI: 10.1002/aris.2009.1440430113 3, 26

Soler, J. M. (2007). Separating the articles of authors with the same name. *Scientometrics*, 72(2):281–290. DOI: 10.1007/s11192-007-1730-z 23, 25, 31

Song, Y., Huang, J., Councill, I. G., Li, J., and Lee Giles, C. (2007). Efficient topic-based unsupervised name disambiguation. In *Proc. of the 7th ACM/IEEE Joint Conference on Digital Libraries*, pages 342–351, Vancouver, BC, Canada. DOI: 10.1145/1255175.1255243 32, 100

Tang, J., Zhang, J., Yao, L., Li, J., Zhang, L., and Su, Z. (2008). ArnetMiner: Extraction and mining of academic social networks. In *Proc. of the 14th ACM SIGKDD International Conference on Knowledge Discovery and Data Mining*, pages 990–998, Las Vegas, NV. DOI: 10.1145/1401890.1402008 88

Torvik, V. I., Weeber, M., Swanson, D. R., and Smalheiser, N. R. (2005). A probabilistic similarity metric for Medline records: A model for author name disambiguation. *Journal of the American Society for Information Science and Technology*, 56(2):140–158. DOI: 10.1002/asi.20105 21, 23, 107

Torvik, V. I. and Smalheiser, N. R. (2009). Author name disambiguation in MEDLINE. *ACM Transactions on Knowledge Discovery from Data*, 3(3):1–29. DOI: 10.1145/1552303.1552304 6, 21, 23, 31, 107

Tran, H. N., Huynh, T., and Do, T. (2014). Author name disambiguation by using deep neural network. In *Asian Conference on Intelligent Information and Database Systems*, pages 123–132, Springer. DOI: 10.1007/978-3-319-05476-6_13 6, 23, 26, 86, 87

Treeratpituk, P. and Lee Giles, C. (2009). Disambiguating authors in academic publications using random Forests. In *Proc. of the ACM/IEEE Joint Conference on Digital Libraries*, pages 39–48, Austin, TX. DOI: 10.1145/1555400.1555408 6, 23, 31

Veloso, A., Ferreira, A. A., Gonçalves, M. A., Laender, A. H. F., and Meira Jr., W. (2012). Cost-effective on-demand associative author name disambiguation. *Information Processing and Management*, 48(4):680–697. DOI: 10.1016/j.ipm.2011.08.005 5, 6, 22, 56

Veloso, A., Meira Jr., W., Cristo, M., Gonçalves, M., and Zaki, M. (2006a). Multi-evidence, multi-criteria, lazy associative document classification. In *Proc. of the ACM CIKM International Conference on Information and Knowledge Management*, pages 218–227, Arlington, VA. DOI: 10.1145/1183614.1183649 53

Veloso, A., Meira Jr., W., and Zaki, M. J. (2006b). Lazy associative classification. In *Proc. of the International Conference on Data Mining*, pages 645–654, Washington, DC. DOI: 10.1109/icdm.2006.96 52

Voulodimos, A., Doulamis, N., Doulamis, A., and Protopapadakis, E. (2018). Deep learning for computer vision: A brief review. *Computational Intelligence and Neuroscience*, 2018(7068349):1–13. DOI: 10.1155/2018/7068349 84

Wang, C., He, X., and Zhou, A. (2020). Heel: Exploratory entity linking for heterogeneous information networks. *Knowledge and Information Systems*, 62(2):485–506. DOI: 10.1007/s10115-019-01354-1 5, 22, 28, 32

Wu, H., Li, B., Pei, Y., and He, J. (2014). Unsupervised author disambiguation using dempster—shafer theory. *Scientometrics*, 101(3):1955–1972. DOI: 10.1007/s11192-014-1283-x 14, 21, 23, 27, 31, 81

Xu, J., Lu, Q., Li, M., and Li, W. (2015). Web person disambiguation using hierarchical co-reference model. In Gelbukh, A., Ed., *Computational Linguistics and Intelligent Text Processing*, pages 279–291, Cham. Springer International Publishing. DOI: 10.1007/978-3-319-18111-0_22 23

Xu, R. and Wunsch, D. (2005). Survey of clustering algorithms. *IEEE Transactions on Neural Networks*, 16:645–678. DOI: 10.1109/tnn.2005.845141 59

Xu, X., Yuruk, N., Feng, Z., and Schweiger, T. A. (2007). SCAN: A structural clustering algorithm for networks. In *Proc. of the 13th ACM SIGKDD International Conference on Knowledge Discovery and Data Mining*, pages 824–833, San Jose, CA. 77, 79 DOI: 10.1145/1281192.1281280

Yang, K.-H., Peng, H.-T., Jiang, J.-Y., Lee, H.-M., and Ho, J.-M. (2008). Author name disambiguation for citations using topic and web correlation. In *Research and Advanced Technology for Digital Libraries, 12th European Conference, ECDL, Proceedings*, pages 185–196, Aarhus, Denmark, September 14-19, Springer-Verlag. DOI: 10.1007/978-3-540-87599-4_19 26, 32

122 BIBLIOGRAPHY

Young, T., Hazarika, D., Poria, S., and Cambria, E. (2018). Recent trends in deep learning based natural language processing [Review Article]. *IEEE Computational Intelligence Magazine*, 13(3):55–75. DOI: 10.1109/mci.2018.2840738 84

Yujian, L. and Bo, L. (2007). A normalized levenshtein distance metric. *IEEE Transactions on Pattern Analysis and Machine Intelligence*, 29(6):1091–1095. DOI: 10.1109/tpami.2007.1078 91

Zaki, M. J. and Meira Jr, W. (2014). *Data Mining and Analysis: Fundamental Concepts and Algorithms*. Cambridge University Press, New York, NY. DOI: 10.1017/cbo9780511810114 26, 27, 28

Zha, H., He, X., Ding, C. H. Q., Gu, M., and Simon, H. D. (2001). Spectral relaxation for K-means clustering. In *Proc. of the 14th International Conference on Neural Information Processing Systems: Natural and Synthetic*, pages 1057–1064, Vancouver, Canada. 28

Zhang, B. and Al Hasan, M. (2017). Name disambiguation in anonymized graphs using network embedding. In *Proc. of the ACM Conference on Information and Knowledge Management*, pages 1239–1248, Singapore. DOI: 10.1145/3132847.3132873 23

Zhang, B., Dundar, M., Dave, V., and Hasan, M. (2019a). Dirichlet process Gaussian mixture for active online name disambiguation by particle filter. In *Proc. of the ACM/IEEE Joint Conference on Digital Libraries*, pages 269–278, Champaign, IL. DOI: 10.1109/jcdl.2019.00045 95

Zhang, S., Xinhua, E., and Pan, T. (2019b). A multi-level author name disambiguation algorithm. *IEEE Access*, 7:104250–104257. DOI: 10.1109/access.2019.2931592 23

Zhang, Y., Zhang, F., Yao, P., and Tang, J. (2018). Name disambiguation in AMiner: Clustering, maintenance, and human in the loop. In *Proc. of the 24th ACM SIGKDD International Conference on Knowledge Discovery and Data Mining*, pages 1002–1011, London, UK. DOI: 10.1145/3219819.3219859 6, 21, 27, 88

Zhao, Z., Rollins, J., Bai, L., and Rosen, G. (2017). Incremental author name disambiguation for scientific citation data. In *Proc. of the 4th IEEE International Conference on Data Science and Advanced Analytics*, pages 175–183, Tokyo, Japan. DOI: 10.1109/dsaa.2017.17 14, 22, 28

Zhou, Q., Liu, Y., Wei, Y., Wang, W., Wang, B., and Wu, S. (2018). Dirichlet process mixtures model based on variational inference for Chinese person name disambiguation. In *Proc. of the International Conference on Computing and Data Engineering*, pages 6–10, Shanghai, China. DOI: 10.1145/3219788.3219803 23

Zhu, J., Wu, X., Lin, X., Huang, C., Fung, G. P. C., and Tang, Y. (2018). A novel multiple layers name disambiguation framework for digital libraries using dynamic clustering. *Scientometrics*, 114(3):781–794. DOI: 10.1007/s11192-017-2611-8 23

Authors' Biographies

ANDERSON A. FERREIRA

Anderson A. Ferreira holds a B.S. degree in Computer Science from the Universidade Federal de Viçosa, Brazil, and an M.Sc. and a Ph.D. degree in Computer Science from the Universidade Federal de Minas Gerais, Brazil, under the supervision of Dr. Marcos André Gonçalves and Prof. Alberto H. F. Laender. In 2011, he joined the Computing Department of the Universidade Federal de Ouro Preto, where he is currently an Associate Professor. He has published several articles in major conferences and journals from the digital libraries and databases areas, such as JCDL, SBBD/JIDM, JASIST, IP&M, DocEng, LA-Web, TKDD, Information Sciences, World Digital, *International Journal on Digital Libraries*, and *SIGMOD Record*. Dr. Ferreira has also served as an ad hoc referee for several journals as *JASIST, Scientometrics, Information Science, The Knowledge Engineering Review, Informetrics, Online Information Review, IP&M, Internet Services and Applications, Machine Learning Research, KNOSYS*, and *Natural Language Engineering*.

MARCOS ANDRÉ GONÇALVES

Marcos André Gonçalves holds a B.S. degree in Computer Science (1995) from the Universidade Federal do Ceará, Brazil, an M.Sc. degree in Computer Science (1997) from the Universidade Estadual de Campinas (UNICAMP), Brazil, and a Ph.D. degree in Computer Science (2004) from Virginia Tech, USA. He joined the Computer Science Department of the Universidade Federal de Minas Gerais in 2005, where he is currently an Associate Professor, coheading the Data Management Research Group along with Prof. Alberto Laender. Dr. Gonçalves has served as a program committee member for several international and national conferences on information retrieval, digital libraries, and Web-related topics, among them: ACM SIGIR, ACM CIKM, ACM/IEEE JCDL, ACM RecSys, TPDL, SBBD, and as reviewer for journals such as *ACM Transactions on Information Systems, Information Processing & Management, Journal of the Association for Information Science*, and *Technology (JASIST), Information Sciences*. He was an Affiliated Member of the Brazilian Academy of Sciences (2008-2012). He has numerous awards including the prestigious Prêmio Capes for Best Brazilian Doctoral Dissertation in Computer Science (co-advisor of Fabiano Belem), awards as advisor for Best Ph.D. Dissertation and Master Thesis from the Brazilian Computer Society (2019, 2018, 2013, 2012), Best Student Paper Award (ACM/IEEE JCDL 2004 and 2014), Prêmio Mauro Castilho–SBBD Best Paper Award (2011, 2010, 2008), and some Google Research Awards (2014–2017). He is the author of more than 300 refereed journal and conference papers. His current research interests include Information Retrieval, Machine Learning, and Social Networks.

ALBERTO H. F. LAENDER

Alberto H. F. Laender holds a B.Sc. degree in Electrical Engineering (1974) and an M.Sc. degree in Computer Science (1979), both from the Universidade Federal de Minas Gerais, Brazil, and a Ph.D. degree in Computing (1984) from the University of East Anglia, UK. He joined the Computer Science Department of the Universidade Federal de Minas Gerais in 1975, where he is a Full Professor and heads the Data Management Research Group. In 1997, he was a Visiting Scholar at HP Labs in Palo Alto, California. He has served on the advisory committee of several Brazilian research funding agencies and was also a member of ACM SIGMOD's Advisory Board (2006-2010) and SIGMOD's Jim Gray Ph.D. Dissertation Award Committee (2008-2011). Prof. Laender has also served as a program committee member for several national and international conferences on databases, digital libraries, and Web-related topics, among them SBBD, KdMiLe, VLDB, CIKM, SIGIR, JCDL, TPDL, WWW, SPIRE and ICDE. He is a founder-member of the Brazilian Computer Society and one of the co-founders of Akwan Information Technologies, a Brazilian search technology company that was acquired by Google Inc. in 2005 to become its Research and Development Center for Latin America. Prof. Laender is a member of the Brazilian Academy of Sciences and of the Brazilian National Academy of Engineering, and in 2010 he was awarded the National Order of the Scientific Merit by the Brazilian President. He is the author of more than 200 refereed journal and conference papers. His current research interests include Data Management, Digital Libraries, Social Networks, and Bibliometrics.

Printed in the United States
by Baker & Taylor Publisher Services